PORTHCAWL
NEWTON AND NOTTAGE
A Concise Illustrated History

by

Alun Morgan, B.A.

Photographs courtesy of Mr Phillip Aspinal
Illustrations and maps by Mrs Margaret Wooding, A.T.D.

1987
D. BROWN AND SONS LIMITED
Cowbridge

© 1987 Alun Morgan, B.A.

ISBN 0 905928 73 3

By the same author
Porthcawl: its History and Development
Legends of Porthcawl and the Glamorgan Coast

Historical Novels
The Breakwater
Inn of Fear
Elizabeth, Fair Maid of Sker
The She Goblin

DESIGNED AND PRINTED IN WALES BY
D. Brown and Sons Ltd., Cowbridge and Bridgend, Glamorgan

Contents

Acknowledgements

Compiling this book would have been impossible without the help of many people and so making distinctions would be invidious; but top of the list of those I wish to thank is Mr. Phillip Aspinal who has generously allowed me free access to his fine collection of photographs of old Porthcawl. Together we have selected items which we thought would appeal most to the general reader and these illustrate the text. I am more than grateful to him. Where no photographs were available or suitable Mrs Margaret Wooding, A.T.D. has once more come to my aid. I thank her for the delightful line-drawings and sketch-maps which grace many of the chapters.

As far as the actual writing is concerned I owe most to Mr Robert Proudfoot who has generously shared with me his encyclopaedic knowledge of the area. He has helped me repeatedly, responding to my requests for information with patience and has frequently gone out of his way to elucidate some obscure matters. I am grateful, too, to Mrs Jill Drew, who provided me with details about her uncle, Mr George Pine, and the Porthcawl 'aerodrome': to Dr. J. H. Thomas, F.R.C.P., who kindly uncovered facts about early Medical Officers of Health: and to Mr Victor Evans, who has researched the history of the 18th Battalion The Welch Regiment (the 'Bantams').

Many societies and institutions have unstintingly made information available to me; and so I have pleasure in thanking the Glamorgan-Gwent Archaeological Trust, Ltd., and especially its Senior Sites and Monuments Officer, Miss Jane Hill-Kann, for providing me with a description of the excavation of the Roman site in the grounds of Dan-y-Graig House; the President and members of the Porthcawl Museum and Historical Society for allowing me access to their now voluminous material; the Board of Management of the Rest Convalescent Home for giving me details of the early Homes; Mr David East, Q.P.M., LL.B., Chief Constable of the South Wales Constabulary, for making it possible for me to obtain information about the police force; and Mr David Newton Williams, B.Arch., F.R.I.B.A., A.I. Arb., Mayor of Porthcawl 1986–87, and Mrs D. Sheppard, Clerk to Porthcawl Town Council, for elucidating certain matters and providing me with a list of the town's clubs and societies.

Finally I wish to record a debt of gratitude to the County Librarian and staff of Mid-Glamorgan County Library, Bridgend. My queries were always answered promptly and I have never ceased to be amazed at the wonderful electronic equipment they have installed, which now makes research so much easier. My thanks, too, go to the staff of Porthcawl County Library, who have frequently and speedily obtained all the books and material I requested.

Preface

'Porthcawl: its History and Development' was written primarily as a guide for the children of local schools in the hope that they would go on to study the history of the area in greater detail. I am pleased to record some success in this direction and am also gratified by the response of Porthcawlians of all ages and especially that of visitors and holiday-makers. It has been suggested that I write a longer history accompanied by many more illustrations and this I have endeavoured to do. I must stress, however, that this book is again aimed at the general reader. Serious students wishing to delve into such complicated matters as the inter-locking estates of the three great manors, the genealogy of the local gentry or the full ramifications of the Brogden family's attempts to turn Porthcawl into a port should consult the late Mr Leonard Higgins' 'Newton, Nottage and Porthcawl'. This book, still available in local libraries, is important not only for its content but also for the copious footnotes which give the author's sources, thus aiding further research. The same writer's 'The Rise and Decline of Porthcawl Docks' (published in 'The Mariner's Mirror', 1964, Vol. 50, No. 4) and 'John Brogden and Sons' (Glamorgan Historian, Vol. 10) should also be read. The Rev. H. Hey Knight's 'Account of Newton-Nottage', which appeared in *Archaeologia Cambrensis* (1853) is worthy of serious study.

I would like to emphasise, too, that the chapters in this book increase in scope and content as they go along. This is because historical knowledge of the area increases as recorded material becomes more readily available; and when the immediate past is dealt with there is an abundance of information, not only written and pictorial but also verbal from older residents, many of whom I have consulted. My own mother, for example, who at the time of writing is in her 99th year, remembers Porthcawl as a young girl, and I myself have lived here for nearly seventy years, so the last century has not been too difficult to deal with.

I have tried to keep the story of Porthcawl and the two villages as concise as possible but there are subjects which, because of the vast amount of information available, are best treated separately. To deal with matters such as education, religion, local government, etc., in the main text would impinge on the narrative, so I have dealt with them in individual chapters towards the end of the book.

Finally it should be remembered that studying the history of the area is like peeling a banana: the outer skin has to come off in all directions before the central core is revealed. This is because before Porthcawl was even a small dot on the maps Newton was in existence, and before Newton there was Nottage. And even before Nottage a prehistoric site was in being on the sandy moorlands of Newton Burrows and Merthyr Mawr Warren. And so we must begin there.

1.

Prehistoric Times

In the *Palaeolithic (Old Stone Age) period* Britain was joined to Europe in a single land mass and the Bristol Channel did not exist. During most of this time Wales was uninhabitable because of a succession of Ice Ages, but in the comparatively warmer periods between the glacial advances primitive hunters followed their prey (which included such animals as mammoths, sabre-toothed tigers and woolly rhinoceros) to the furthest reaches of the land. The nearest evidence that such a people came to this region is to be found in the Paviland Cave on the Gower Peninsula, where the skeleton of a young man was found. The weapons they used were wooden spears tipped with chipped stones or bones and clumsy stone axes. They probably dug trapping pits with the shoulder bones of larger animals.

Between 8000 and 2500 B.C. (*the Mesolithic or Middle Stone Age period*) there was a downward movement of the land and the Bristol Channel was formed. It was narrower than it is now and at the same time the weather became warmer. The hunters in this area became fishermen as well, for the finding of small stone implements known as megaliths (used as harpoons, scrapers and borers) on Merthyr Mawr Warren suggest that their main diet was now fish and shellfish. These people progressed very little and their existence on the warren must have been miserable. Attempts to better and improve life did not come until the *Neolithic (New Stone Age)* period, lasting from about 3000 to 2000 B.C., when a new race of people came from the continent bringing with them a higher standard of living. Some of these people, too, settled in the Merthyr Mawr area. Their weapons were made of polished flint, the arrow- and axe-heads in particular being finely made to fit sockets in wood. They knew how to grow crops, and kilns found in the area suggest that they burnt sea-weed to use as a fertilizer. They began to use domestic animals and made a rough form of pottery; and no longer were they content to use caves, making proper homes for themselves known as pit-dwellings. Sometimes they improved the structures by building circular stone walls. A good example of such a house has been found near Mount Pleasant farm at Tŷ Coch, unusual in being an above-ground dwelling and not constructed around a pit. It is remarkable, too, that these people must have believed in some form of after-life, for they made many of their best structures to shelter their dead. These burial chambers, known as long barrows, are to be found all over the region, the nearest one being at Tythegston, just off the A4106. The best example, big enough to hold many bodies together with domestic animals, can be seen at Tinkinswood, near Cardiff.

Soon after 2000 B.C., when the *Bronze Age* in the British Isles is considered to have started, groups of newcomers arrived from Spain, bringing with them the art of metal making. The material they used was bronze, a mixture of one tenth

HOUSES FOR THE LIVING—

1a   Pit dwelling

-AND FOR THE DEAD

1b   Round barrow

tin and nine tenths copper, smelted in ordinary wood fires. They were called
Beaker Folk, so named because they made decorated pots, marked in a distinc-
tive way. Using their better weapons they were able to clear parts of the forests
(then universal throughout the land) and became good farmers. They, too,
buried their dead (the more important chieftains at least) but now the bodies
were placed in single graves under circular mounds (Round Barrows). An even
firmer belief in an after-life is is indicated by the fact that the bodies were placed
sometimes in a sitting, sometimes in a crouched position, together with such
things as weapons and beakers. Many of these burial chambers exist in and
around Porthcawl. There was one at Locks Lane and another on the path
connecting West Road and Rest Bay, both now sadly obliterated by the
advance of housing. Also obliterated is a barrow (interestingly found to the
north of a field called The Barrow) near Nottage, which was disturbed when
the railway tunnel under the village was being excavated in the middle of the
nineteenth century. It contained a skeleton showing all the signs of a careful
burial. A cairn at Stormy Down was examined in 1928, revealing a crouched
skeleton of a male lying on its side, with evidence suggesting that it was a
Beaker burial; and in March 1973 a mechanical excavator went through the
roof of a tomb half a mile from the sea on Newton Burrows. The chamber
contained a skeleton in a good state of preservation with only a few bones
missing, and in the usual crouched position, leading Dr. Savory to the conclusion that this, too, had been a Beaker burial. There were also within or near the
parish other elements who cremated their dead and placed cinerary urns in their
graves. The area around Merthyr Mawr and Candleston is especially rich in
burial mounds and many artefacts have been found there, especially after storms
have disturbed the sand. In the absence of sufficient cash to investigate the
moorland thoroughly it is hoped that any future industrial work (such as the
proposed laying of a sewage pipe between Porthcawl and Ogmore) will yield
other finds. If the workmen are warned to be careful and observant there may
be rich rewards. Other finds suggest that Bronze Age people lived in small
groups all round the area: for example an axe head at Rest Bay and a spear head
on the Royal Porthcawl Golf Club course.

Before leaving the Bronze Age period it should be mentioned that the people
who lived here were part of the greater family of Celts who were responsible
for the commencement of Stonehenge on Salisbury Plain. From their vantage
points on the hills and sand dunes the local tribes would have seen rafts, so
heavily laden as to be almost out of view, being rowed along by their fellow
countrymen. The rafts held the huge blue stones that had been quarried in the
Prescelly Mountains, now destined to form the inner ring of that mysterious
construction.

The last invasion of our island before recorded history began came about 500
B.C. when Celtic tribes, driven from the Rhineland by fierce German warriors,
started to arrive on the south and east coasts. They quickly conquered or
intermingled with the earlier Bronze Age Celts and one tribe, the Silures,
settled in Glamorganshire. This was the start of the *Iron Age*.

2 Celtic shield

We cannot tell exactly when iron-making began for bronze and iron were used side by side for many years, but the newcomers had mastered the art of the furnace and were therefore able to obtain the greater heat required for smelting. They could turn out excellent implements and weapons, brought to perfection later by a style of ironcraft called La Tène. Bowls, tankards, mirrors and finely decorated plaques and shields were their principal products, all of a design and finish which compels admiration even by modern man.

It was the finding of a La Tène brooch by the late Mr and Mrs G. E. Blundell of Nottage Court which led to the discovery of a settlement site on Merthyr Mawr Warren. Three mounds were excavated by Sir Cyril Fox, who concluded that between 400 and 300 B.C. the area was covered with sand to a depth of between 3ft. and 6 ft., and that the people who lived there worked in both bronze and iron. They were still hunters but they also possessed domesticated animals, and added to their diet by fishing. Their pottery was poor but undoubtedly they heated their water and cooked their food by means of pot-boilers.

The fact that some Iron Age people settled in the Merthyr Mawr area is interesting, for their speciality was the building of hill forts and the terrain did not possess the big, flat-topped elevations necessary for such works. If they built such structures no trace of them remains today, although there is a likely site on Stormy Down which has not yet been excavated. One thing we are sure of, however: these people were our true ancestors, the real Ancient Britons who were soon to meet the might of the Roman Empire. They took over the existing Stonehenge, enlarged it and probably used it for worship of the sun. Some historians believe they carried out human sacrifice there; but whether they did or not the Druidical circle of stone has become part of the tradition of our National Eisteddfod.

2.

The Romans

In 55 B.C. and a year later Julius Caesar led punitive and exploratory raids on Britain, but the resistance of the fierce Celtic tribes was such that a permanent settlement was not planned, and Britain was left alone for a further ninety eight years. But in A.D. 43 the Romans came to conquer and, aided by the old Celtic weaknesses of jealousy and inter-tribal rivalry, quickly established themselves in the south. The British chieftain Caradoc fled to the Silures in South Wales but had little respite for within four years the Romans were entering Wales via the River Severn.

Caerleon was built as a base and the Roman attack came along the most obvious route—from the east along the lowlands between the mountains and sea. In the wake of the legionaries came the roads, planned as straight as possible. From Cardiff, where the Romans built a fort, the road ran due west across Stalling Down at Cowbridge (where its construction can be examined today), and then on towards the base of Crack Hill on the present A 48. From there its route has not definitely been determined, but it is thought to have crossed the River Ogmore either at Bridgend or Ewenny. The latter place seems the more likely, for it is here that the old coaching road had a ford (the passengers changing carriages there) and such routes often followed the Roman example which already had a firm base. From there it probably traversed Stormy Down, reappearing again along Heol y Sheet and Water Street, where Roman military stones have been found. So there can be little doubt about one thing: the road must have passed very close to the northern boundary of our parish. This raises the intriguing mystery of a missing Roman fort in this area.

The Romans built these forts usually eighteen or nineteen miles apart, which was considered to be the most suitable distance for a legionary to march in one day. We know that there was a fort at Cardiff and one at Neath, so the question arises: where was the one in between? The Romans referred to it as Bomium and Cowbridge has been suggested as its possible site, especially as recent excavations have revealed abundant traces of Roman occupation there. But Cowbridge is too near Cardiff, so the fort could well have been near Bridgend or Ewenny, or even possibly on Stormy Down. In the absence of definite proof, which may well yet appear, we can only conjecture, but it is a possibility that the fort was not far from Porthcawl.

In this connection a second conundrum appears. Old maps refer to a site near the Royal Porthcawl club house which is called Castell Morlais. The word Morlais is also referred to as Môr Llais which, being literally translated (a poetic connotation perhaps) means Sea-voice or Sea-sound. The derivation of the name is obscure, for the correct version should be Llais y Môr, but there is no doubt about Castell, which comes from the Latin 'castellum' meaning fort. Such names do not come about by chance, so there may very well have been a fort there, and Mr Robert Proudfoot, who has made a detailed study of Nottage and its environs, states that when he was working on an extension to the clubhouse he came across the remains of an old wall where the foundations of the present structure had been excavated. The Rev. H. Hey Knight refers to a ruined cottage there, so once again there can only be conjecture. In any case, if

3 The Royal Porthcawl Golf Club pavilion, erected on land called Castell Morlais. See Chapter 2

there had been a fort on the site it was probably merely a look-out or signal tower, for it is too far away from the Via Maritima to be the missing Bomium.

One thing is certain. Finds in the area had already shown the presence of a Roman or Romano-British culture. A brass face of Medusa was discovered at the foot of an old wall to the north of Nottage Court and a coin of a Roman Empress in an earth bank at Dan-y-Graig House, a manor house built about 1817 on the site of a previous seventeenth or eighteenth century dwelling. This latter find gave rise to speculation that a Roman or Romano-British villa existed on the site and so, after some preliminary exploration work, the Glamorgan-Gwent Archaeological Trust started a 'dig' there in 1986. I am indebted to Miss Jan Hill-Kann, Senior Sites and Monuments Officer of the Trust, who provided me with information about the excavation work, which I summarize here:

Two trial sections had already been excavated. One produced little evidence but the more northerly revealed the remains of a wall of Roman date and part of a T-shaped corn drier. Material used in landscaping the present house (now a Senior Citizens' Home) had been used to fill in a ha-ha (a sunken boundary fence) which ran diagonally across the site and cut through deposits of Roman destruction debris. This debris had been levelled off to form a metalled surface, and in this area were the trenches of a Roman building. There were also eight post-holes of varying sizes in no discernible pattern. Two of these cut into a surface of fist-sized stones and hard core containing burnt bones, and another into second or third century pottery. In another hole were shards of coarse ware, again of the second or third centuries. The walls of the building were approximately 0.9 metres wide and well-constructed of mortar and carboniferous limestone. The interior of the building had a partially metalled floor, the rest being made of compacted clay. Under the clay, and immediately adjacent to the building, was a T-shaped drying kiln. Under debris found in the kiln a large amount of cereal grain and a third-century radiate coin were discovered.

Removal of the metalled surface revealed fourteen further post-holes, again of no coherent pattern. The conclusion reached was that the structure investigated was possibly a Roman corn barn. That a dwelling house or houses were located nearby was indicated by large quantities of painted wall plaster in the debris. The location of this building (or buildings) would appear to be to the west of the excavated area within a field currently under pasture, where low earth-works were noted. It is believed that these are indicative of a villa complex.

So the conjecture of many years has at last been substantiated, and it is gratifying to know that there really was a Roman presence in the parish; and for that we must be grateful to the archaeologists who toiled so hard at the site. This happy knowledge permits us now to go on with the general story, essential if we are to understand what happened next in the area.

For a long time Britain enjoyed relative peace and prosperity behind the shield of the legionary. There was inter-marriage between conqueror and conquered and the Welsh language gained from an influx of Latin words, for example ffenestr (window) from fenestra, melin (mill) from molina and porth (gate or port) from porta. But the period of law and order was not to last, for in the fifth century Barbarian hordes were attacking the Roman Empire in strength. The legions had to withdraw to defend the homeland, leaving Britain open to attack by fierce Germanic tribes known as Angles, Saxons and Jutes. Fortunately for Wales the enemy found the Welsh mountains too intimidating, for they stopped short at the foothills. King Offa built his famous dyke (more of a boundary than a line of defence) and from then on the two countries took on identifiable forms: England (Angleland) and the Cymry (fellow-countrymen, a word indicating the unity of the Brythons of Wales with their fellow Celts of the North.)

The British fought hard against the invader, as Saxon chronicles show, and one chieftain, Arthur, succeeded in uniting the Celtic tribes in their fierce opposition. Whether or not he was buried in a ruined chapel near Pencoed (a claim put forward but not yet proved to the satisfaction of eminent historians) it should be remembered that the picture of him as a knight in shining armour is false, as are the stories of his leading twelve other knights in a constant search for the Holy Grail and beautiful damsels in distress—a pet aversion of historians and history teachers. The horse he rode was a small pony and if he wore armour it was probably a discarded Roman breastplate; and his soldiers were unruly tribesmen wearing roughly-woven clothes. If there was such a place as Camelot, Arthur did not have much spare time to tarry there, for he was constantly pressed and harried by the enemy. Alfred, Lord Tennyson has much to answer for. We do know, however, that the Britons eventually succumbed and a stream of refugees entered Wales and Cornwall, which became known as West Wales. These two regions then entered a period of comparative isolation and, because of the Roman heritage of Christianity, developed an individual church of their own. This church, known as the Celtic Church, gave birth to a long line of men who became regarded as saints, the most famous being St. David, who is reputed to have studied at a monastic settlement based in Llantwit Major. Whether or not he started a cell near here we do not know, but it is believed that there was a chapel at Nottage at this time, a belief strengthened by the nearby presence of a holy well named after him. Active near here, too, was St. Cornelius who, according to legend, lived a hermit-like life in a cave near Cornelly. He was the patron Saint of horned cattle and even today a feast is held in his honour in Brittany, another Celtic region.

Wales at this time was therefore a bastion of Christianity against the heathen invaders who, it has already been stated, stopped short at the border. But the Saxons pushed forward in great numbers along routes leading to what is today the West Country, stopping only at the River Tamar. From their vantage points on the hills and moorlands of Devon and Somerset they could see Wales across the Bristol Channel, an inviting target for the more daring. Raiding parties in flat-bottomed boats set out to explore parts of the South Wales coast, and this brings us to the question of Nottage.

3.

Saxons, Vikings and Nottage

Some historians have suggested that the original name of Nottage was Llan-ddewi and that the village was the site of an early Celtic settlement built around or near a chapel. The Welsh word 'llan' means an enclosed space, but over the centuries came to depict a church as well (understandable because all the early chapels were built in clearings in the forests then covering Wales); and Dewi is the Welsh form of David. This supposition is sound for there is a holy well on the outskirts of the village called St David's Well, and legend has it that St David himself or possibly one of the hermit-saints who abounded in great numbers in the fifth and sixth centuries had a cell there. Interestingly the hollow in which the well is situated also has a connotation with the patron saint, being called Dewiscumbe. If such a cell or chapel had existed there would be no trace of it today, for all such places were made of wood: but there seems little doubt that there was some sort of religious settlement nearby. In 1851 the remains of an early Christian burial and fragments of a village cross were found near Siop-y-Groes (the Shop of the Cross); and a 1630 survey of Pembroke Manor and an even earlier Manorial Rent Roll refer to the presence of a chapel. Finally, a purchase deed of Tŷ Talbot farm dated 1785 mentions one of the buildings as being a church situated on land now occupied by Ashcott Villa, near the Rose and Crown Inn. (The site was disturbed when the railway tunnel was being built and found to contain many human bones). The street called Heol-y-Capel (Road of the Chapel) is thought to have been a pilgrim's way leading from the church to the holy well. Equally possible, of course, is the suggestion that the site was occupied by a monastic chapel associated with Noge Court Grange, a wheat farm owned by the monks of Margam Abbey. There is no means of telling which it was; but there can be no doubt that Nottage possessed an ancient church which was subsequently abandoned when the Normans built Newton and St John's church. The Normans, being of the Catholic faith, would have had no truck with the earlier Celtic church and its myriad of saints.

But the name Llanddewi has been lost to antiquity and bears no resemblance to the present name Nottage, and so we must start all over again. The village has been referred to at various times in old maps and documents as Nothasse, Notaissh, Notashe and Notesash, and there is a Welsh form, Notais, as is shown in a sixteenth century document which called it 'Y Dre Newydd yn Notais' (the New Town in Nottage). There has been much speculation about the name. Originally it was thought to have derived from the Norse, or Scandinavian, meaning 'an ash grove by the boathouse', but this is not now generally accepted. Mr B. G. Charles, in his 'Non-Celtic Place Names in Wales', shows conclusively that it stems from the Old English 'hnot', meaning 'the pollard ash tree', and mentions that there are many places in Saxon England with the name Nottage. This conclusion is supported by the fact that the name Dewiscumbe, already mentioned, is a mixture of Welsh and Old English; and so there seems little doubt that the village had some sort of Saxon connection. The puzzle is how this came about for we know that the original Saxons who occupied Devon and Somerset raided the Welsh coast but they were never allowed to settle, being chased by the local chieftains either back across the water or up into the hills. There can be only one possible explanation. The Saxons were good farmers and after they had settled down some of them became traders. They may therefore have used Nottage as a trading post towards the end of the eighth century—at a time when they were being given a taste of their own medicine by the Vikings. The Norsemen carved out a huge area for themselves in England called Danelaw and then began terrorising the Bristol Channel area. In the face of the common enemy the Welsh of Wales and Cornwall and the Saxons of Wessex, fighting desperately under Alfred the Great, may have found some form of rapport for their mutual good. But all this is conjecture, which led Mr Leonard Higgins to reach the only safe conclusion he could arrive at: that Nottage village was a pre-Norman settlement.

We are on safer ground when we study the movement of the Vikings. With colonies already set up in Ireland they lost no time in raiding the west coast of Britain and the Bristol Channel area. This particular branch of Norsemen, known as Black Pagans, explored every inlet and river on the South Wales coast, and we know how active they were from their place-names. They formed settlements at Sker (Scandinavian for jagged reef), Sweyn See (the homestead of Sweyn—now Swansea), Monknash, Nash and Wick. They enjoyed making use of islands and any bit of land that protruded from the sea, such as Skomer, Skokholm, Tuskar, Flat Holm and Steep Holm; and their flat-bottomed boats made it possible for them to raid far inland.

Unfortunately for the inhabitants of Nottage (or Llanddewi) the settlement lay at the head of just the type of creek the Vikings favoured, running from the sea to the base of the hill on which the dwellings stood; and there can be little doubt that the raiders made use of it. Using bore-holes, Mr G. E. Blundell succeeded in determining its route. Starting near a depression to the east of the village called the Rhyll the stream passed close to the site of Ffynnon Fawr (near the Nottage roundabout) and entered the lakes and wet-lands of The Wilderness. From there it went in a southerly direction through what is known today as the Salt Lake car park, previously the inner harbour of the old dock, and entered the sea somewhere along Coney Beach. This stream now appears to have gone underground, a fact that can be ascertained today by looking at the considerable amount of water which, even in times of long and severe drought, never ceases to flow through holes and cracks in the northern wall of the outer harbour. This tidal estuary, not then impeded by modern structures and roads, was undoubtedly the route taken by the marauders. Two other facts strengthen the likelihood of this having happened. In the marshy area called The Wilderness are Standing Stones. Of great antiquity (they were probably there long

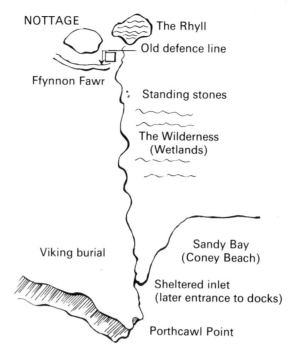

4   Sketch Map showing possible route of the stream that ran from Nottage to the coast

before the Viking era) one of them is worn around the middle, giving every indication that it had once been used as a mooring post. Then, in 1846 what is thought to have been a Viking grave was unearthed near the present Fulgoni's cafe (the one near the police station). There, encased in stonework which could only have come from Devon or Somerset (where the Vikings also made settlements) an urn was found containing human remains which had been burned with a mixture of sods and brushwood—a typical Scandinavian burial.

Finally there is the appearance of Nottage itself. The entire village was constructed with defence in mind, with narrow, confusing lanes (still narrow and confusing today) bounded by dwellings, including long houses, placed so that their ends abutted the thoroughfares, all intended to give an enemy a hard time of it if he breached the outer defences. These outer defences, consisting of a ditch and boundary line of some strength, lay on the verge of the south-west slope. (When Locks Lane was constructed the roadway had to be raised to cross this defence-line.) All this, plus a natural defensive position on a hillock, points to the influence of the Vikings who, being sea raiders themselves, knew how to make their homesteads safe against further attack from the sea. This does not mean that the present cottages and dwellings of Nottage were in existence at that time—the Vikings favoured wood as building material—but later houses probably follow the original plan. What is certain is that any previous inhabitants would have been massacred or forced to flee inland.

Eventually, of course, the Vikings in Wales, like all the other Norse people in Britain, became Christian, and so in a way Nottage came round full circle. St Augustine succeeded in converting the heathens of England, forming the Catholic Church which was later joined to the older Celtic Church. Angles, Saxons, Jutes and Vikings turned to the less-warlike pursuits of farming and trading, as did their compatriots who had gained a foothold on Welsh soil. Such a man as Lales, who started the settlement known as Laleston, may have taught the earlier inhabitants the skills of strip-farming, a method of agriculture which was to remain in being for several hundred years, and it is very likely that Nottage as well had become a farming community before the end of the tenth century.

The Vikings were not yet finished with Britain, however. Their descendants, the Normans (another word for Northmen) were still to complete the last successful invasion of the country; and the existing inhabitants, already a mixture of Celts, Romans, Angles, Saxons and Scandinavians, were eventually exposed to a new continental influence, the French. And that leads directly to the story of Newton.

4.

Newton and the Normans

If the antiquity of Nottage leaves us in doubt as to its true origins there is no mystery about Newton. First, the general background. In 1066 William, Duke of Normandy, landed on Pevensey Beach near the present town of Hastings, intent on wresting the crown from the English King Harold. After the famous battle, on the site of which the commemorative Abbey was built, the Normans lost no time in subjugating the rest of England, and when they had succeeded in that they turned their attention to Wales. The knight entrusted with the assault was Robert Fitzhamon.

The first attack, as with all other invasions, came along the South Wales coast. As soon as land was occupied, the Normans built quickly-constructed castles for immediate defence. Such castles (given the name Motte and Bailey— see diagram) could be constructed in a few weeks, the labourers usually being local people given the choice of either raising the mounds or being used for target practice by the long-bow men. One of Fitzhamon's underlings, Baron de Sturmi, came to our area and built a Motte and Bailey at Stormy Down, just off the present A48, so the Down is named after a knight and not because it is particularly stormy. Fitzhamon also built a similar castle at Kenfig, probably on

5   Motte and Bailey Castle

the site of a defence-work raised by the defeated Welsh Lord, Iestyn ap Cwrgan, and later converted it into a proper stone castle called a Shell Keep. Skilfully sited so that it had a clear view along the flat land to the west and down the lower reaches of the River Kenfig, then navigable as far as the sea, it formed the nucleus of a future Norman town. Another bastion, hemming in our parish on the eastern side, was constructed near the confluence of the Ogmore and Ewenny rivers. Ogmore castle was placed in the keeping of William de Londres, the fiercest and most capable of Fitzhamon's knights, and seems to have been built of stone from the beginning. In a comparatively short time, therefore, our forebears living in this area found themselves in a stranglehold, and it was soon apparent that resistance against the harsh, militant knights and their soldiers was useless.

To give thanks to God for their success the Normans turned, as soon as they were able, to the building of abbeys and churches. In 1147 the Cistercian abbey of Margam was founded, and some time between that date and 1183 a grant of land was given by William, Earl of Gloucester (the grandson of Robert Fizhamon) to Richard de Cardiff. This grant of land, described in the deeds then drawn up as 'Novam Villam in Margan' (Margan being a corruption of Morgan) was the beginning of Newton village. The name Novam Villam (New Town) itself indicates that there was an older settlement nearby which, of course, was Nottage. Unfortunately there is no record of the exact extent of the land, but it appears to have been much larger than the present parish, incorporating Pyle, parts of Kenfig Hill and Sker (the latter later to be the subject of bitter litigation involving the church.)

As with every other township they created, the Normans soon turned their attention to the building of a church. There is doubt as to when exactly Newton church was started. Some historians believe the edifice was commenced by Richard de Cardiff himself; others think that it was founded by the Norman crusading Knights of the Order of St. John of Jerusalem, the driving force being another knight called de Sanford. The evidence seems to favour the latter, after whom the nearby holy well was first named, and also by the fact that the church is dedicated to St. John. There is no means of telling, but it is safe to assume that the church was built some time between the end of the twelfth century and the beginning of the thirteenth. The present structure was largely re-built in the fifteenth century (between 1485 and 1495) and is thought to have been the work of Jasper Tudor, Duke of Bedford and uncle of Henry VII, who later held the Lordship of Glamorgan. The chancel also appears to have been renovated in the sixteenth century, but enough of the structure remains to show that the church, like most early Norman churches, was built to act also as a fortress. The squat, battlemented tower with its narrow windows to aid archers is indicative of this, and the building itself would have acted as a look-out against attack from the sea. Perhaps the most remarkable item in the church is the semi-circular stone pulpit with its surface depicting the flagellation of Christ, unusual in being shown beardless, a fact that led the Rev. R Knight, Vicar of Tewkesbury, to suggest (in 1812) that the church was built on or near one of even greater antiquity.

As with all Norman settlements a township developed around the church, and Newton grew steadily in size. The fields around were given over to the manorial system of farming, with its fair but wasteful allocation of strips. This method was in use only in the lowlands of Wales (called Bro Morgannwg), where the Norman writ ran. In the hilly areas (Blaenau Morgannwg) the Welsh chieftains were largely left to their own devices. Aerial photographs have shown that the open fields lay at the foot of the Tŷ-Coch and Dan-y-Graig ridge, a fact that can be substantiated today by observing the way lanes such as Zig-Zag (previously known as Heol-y-Brittons Way) continuously twist and turn, following the original routes between the old, carefully laid out strips. The land to the south of these fields was too sandy for the good cultivation of crops; and the area to the north (on top of the ridge) was designated as common land and reserved for grazing. Later a windmill was built there, for there were no streams in the parish large enough to drive a water mill, and the site on top of the ridge was ideal to catch the prevailing winds. The ruins of the mill can be seen today.

The question of land-ownership was paramount to the Norman feudal system, and unluckily for Richard de Cardiff he had no son but left two daughters, Amabel and Hardwise. Amabel married Sir Thomas de Sanford (already referred to in connection with the holy well); and in 1197, the year her father died, the estate was bequeathed to her. This raised an immediate difficulty, for under Norman law in the absence of a male heir the land should have been divided between the female issue, a requirement further complicated by

6 The pulpit in Newton Church depicting the flagellation of Christ

the fact that the original grant of land was but a quarter fee, the rest being retained by William, Earl of Gloucester. There followed transfers of land and parcels of land so complicated that only an earnest student of history would have the courage to try and follow the ramifications; for the general reader it is easier to remember that, because of the lines of descent in the ruling families, the lands of the parish of Newton-Nottage took on the names of the eventual holders, finally becoming known as the Pembroke Manor, the Lougher Manor and the Herbert Manor, all families who had vast estates in other parts of the country. However, for those who wish to delve deeper into the subject, here is a short summary of what eventually came about.

Half of Richard de Cardiff's quarter fee ultimately passed into the hands of the de Turbervilles of Tythegston and then by marriage to the Loughers of Sker. This estate became known as the *Lougher Manor*. The other half of the quarter fee (with Candleston) passed eventually to Sir Mathew Cradock and then, again by marriage, to the Herberts of Swansea, after which it was known as the *Herbert Manor*. The three-quarters of the original fee, which remained with the lordship of Glamorgan, passed successively through the hands of the de Clares, Despensers, Beauchamps and Nevilles, eventually ending up being returned to the King, then Richard III. After Bosworth it went to Henry VII and was granted in 1550 to Sir William Herbert, who became Earl of Pembroke, and so his lands were called the *Pembroke Manor*.

To complicate matters still further, no early map showing the precise boundaries of these estates in Newton-Nottage exists, and subsequent quarrels over possession were bitter and long-lasting. For example, a dispute between Watkin Lougher, who held what became the Lougher Manor, and Sir William Herbert over Merthyr Mawr Warren (including the track which then ran between Newton and Ogmore and a house called Little Wick standing on the site of the present Wig Fach farm) began in 1568 and lasted thirty years—good for the lawyers but not for the litigants. In other disputes the jurors were continually confused because the land was "so intricatlie mixed" that decisions were either put back for years or shelved altogether. Complicated though this subject is, it is worth remembering that the tenanted land of the parish was divided between the Pembroke, Lougher and Herbert Manors in the ratios of approximately 3.8: 3.1: 1. This knowledge will help to explain the development of land-tenure, dealt with in later chapters.

5.

The Middle Ages

The period between the eleventh and fifteenth centuries is known as the Middle Ages, and during this period the Norman overlords, although retaining a tight grip on their suzerainty and domains, often married Welsh women of princely descent. Mixed marriages also became the norm with their soldiers and retainers, and so Britain as a whole gradually took on the form it is today. It is worth remembering, too, that the language of the conquerors eventually succumbed to the language of the conquered, with the result that English, albeit now heavily laced with French words, became the predominant tongue in England and many of the parts of Wales conquered by the Normans.

At the beginning of this period the old village of Nottage and the newer village of Newton were overshadowed by a larger and more important area of population—the city of Kenfig. The name is thought to have derived from either Cefn-y-ffignon, a corruption meaning a ridge on a marsh, or Cen-y-fig, Welsh for head of the swamp. In this marshy area a town grew up near Fitzhamon's castle (the remains of which can still be seen today) and quickly attained a degree of importance—'a town for marchandize upon the sea bankes of Kynfege.' There were frequent raids by the disinherited Welsh Lords of Afon, especially Morgan Gam, and the town was burned down so often the citizens built a stockade around the perimeter. In spite of the attacks the town grew steadily in size, and by a Royal Charter its burgesses were allowed to levy their own taxes and make their own by-laws. The town had a High Street into which 'noe butchers shal cast noe heads, feet nor non other garbage', and there were strict ordinances governing food, drink, weights and measures.

For a time Kenfig was a busy market town drawing in the produce of the surrounding area, including that of the yeomen farmers of Newton and Nottage. It is not difficult to imagine them taking their wares there, travelling on foot across the moors and frequently returning in darkness. Moors at night, especially in highly superstitious times, are a certain prescription for belief in the supernatural, and the area abounded in stories of ghosts and goblins. There was, for example, the Gwrach y Rhibyn (the Hag of the Mists); the dreaded White Horse which, if encountered on a night of full moon, meant the certain death of the beholder; the ubiquitous Bwci Bo (a mischievous hob-goblin) and the Cyhiraeth, a ghostly wailing or shrieking sound which was the harbinger of a wreck or storm. In the town itself the farmers would have been prey to the blandishments of mendicants selling pieces of wood purported to be from the Cross or phials of the blood of Christ, actually pig's blood; and they would have heard news of happenings in the outside world, such as the carnage of the Black Death and the Hundred Years War against France, in which the English armies were successful largely because of the courage and skill of Welsh archers.

7 St David's Well, Nottage

There seems little doubt that had Kenfig gone on growing in size it would eventually have swallowed up both Nottage and Newton, but the enemy was sand. A series of typhoon-like storms beginning about 1300, interspersed with long periods of shifting sand, gradually buried the city and made life impossible for the inhabitants; and by the sixteenth century it was, according to Leland, nothing more 'than a little village on the est side of Kenfik and a castel both in ruine and shokid and devoured with the Sandes that the Severn Se there castith up.' The storms also raised up a surrounding ridge of sandhills, with the result that the marsh gradually became a lake of between seventy and eighty acres about 1000 yards from the sea. Fed by underground springs the fresh water of Kenfig Pool has given rise to several legends, the principal one being that the ruined buildings and church tower of the old town can be seen just below the surface. This is not true, for we know that they were sited to the south of the castle walls, at least half a mile from the Pool.

Newton and Nottage were therefore left to grow at their own pace, which was pitifully slow because of heavy and early mortality. The majority of children died in infancy and very few adults lived to be forty. Life went on revolving around the church and the land, a synopsis played out in every area conquered by the Normans and their descendants. The two villages did have one asset in common, however, that raised them above the ordinary, and that was the possession of no less than three holy or healing wells.

Probably the oldest is *St David's Well*, situated in Moor Lane, just outside Nottage. Because of the name the well has been associated with a nearby chapel of the Celtic Church but, as has already been pointed out, there is no firm evidence of this. Equally well there could have been a nearby cell belonging to the monks or lay monks who farmed the Noge Court Grange owned by Margam Abbey. What is certain is that from earliest times the water of the well has been regarded as having curative properties, a belief that prompted Dr Hartland, a well-known local physician in the nineteen twenties and thirties, to advocate its use for all manner of complaints, principally rheumatism, haemorrhoids and skin disorders. It should be pointed out that the water has been analysed in recent years and found to be no better and no worse than ordinary tap water, but such is the power of auto-suggestion that many people claimed relief or even complete cure.

Nottage also boasts a second well, known as *Ffynnon Fawr*, situated just outside the walls of Nottage Court near the Nottage roundabout. This was reputed to have the clearest and best-tasting water of all three wells, and its prodigious output encouraged the laying of pipes to the houses of an early and growing Porthcawl, a system used for many years before the advent of proper tap water. So famous did it become that the wall housing it was inscribed with verses in Welsh, one of which reads as follows:

Mae Dwr yn fendith angenreidol
Rhoddes Duw inni ar lawr;
Cofiwn 'Awdur pob daioni'
Wrth yfed Dwr o'r Ffynnon Fawr.

The approximate translation of this is:

> Water is a necessary blessing which God has given us on earth; Let us remember 'the Author of all goodness' as we drink from Fynnon Fawr.

The best known well, one that was regarded in the Middle Ages as being magical as well as holy, is *St John's Well*, situated about a hundred yards to the south of the church. Originally called Sanford's Well, after the Norman Knight of that name, it early gained a reputation for having curative properties. The magical side stemmed from an apparent anomaly: the well seemed to be empty when the tide on nearby Newton beach was in and full when the tide was out. Blackmore wrote: 'The children are all a little afraid of it, partly because of its maker's name ... and partly on account of its curious ways, and the sand coming out of its "nostrils" when first it begins to flow.' We know the reason for this today: the inflow of fresh water from underground springs is affected by subterranean passages connecting the well with the beach. These passages contain fissures that act like valves, drawing the water away by vacuum as the tide rises, and allowing it to re-enter the well as it recedes. But in the Middle Ages this phenomenon was regarded as being supernatural, causing people to scourge themselves there to atone for their sins. The belief in the curative properties of the water was given an impetus in recent times by the afore-mentioned Dr. Hartland, who discovered that the well emptied part of its contents on to Newton Beach, so he set up an open-air spa there, complete with a large stone slab, to hold the many utensils people brought in the hope of curing their ailments. Sad to relate this water, too, has been analysed and found to be nothing out of the ordinary, but Dr. Hartland's stone dispensing slab can still be seen on the beach.

Near the well an enclosure was maintained solely for the purpose of burning a bonfire. This was an annual event, usually held on Mid-summer's day, the object being to ensure a good harvest, and is thought to have its origins in the ancient druidical rites of Bâltan, named after Bêl or Beli, the Celtic god of light. The rites included leaping over the fire on the part of the younger members of the community, and the embers were carefully preserved to start the next year's fire. Later the bonfire was moved to the village green, where it eventually became synonymous with the celebration of the burning of Guy Fawkes. The fires grew so big they became a menace to life and property, and so were discontinued.

There was also a belief at this time that the sea would eventually return to St John's Well, coming along the creek which then existed along the route of what is today Beach Road. When this took place, villagers believed, it would be possible for a ship to be moored at the base of Clevis Hill. For this reason a sycamore tree was planted on the highest point of the hill. The name Clevis is interesting. Referred to in old documents as 'the Clieves', it is thought by some to have derived from Glywys, which was the name of one of the four sons of a Welsh chieftain who conquered Glamorgan between 460 and 470 in the wake of the Roman withdrawal. This seems to support the belief, long held, that a Welsh prince had a dwelling near the site of the present Dan-y-Graig House.

For convenience historians regard 1485 as the year marking the end of the Middle ages and the beginning of 'Modern Times'. In that year a man of Welsh descent, Henry Tudor, landed near Milford Haven and marched with a growing army to a place called Bosworth, where he defeated Richard III and placed the crown of England on his own head. Henry named his eldest son Arthur, after the Celtic chieftain who had fought so hard against the Saxons, and it seemed that the old Welsh prophecy of a return to greatness under the reincarnation of their hero was about to come true. Fortunately for us this was the time of the start of proper records, for the Tudors wanted to know everything about their new dominions, thus making it easier for present-day historians. Happily many of the documents dealing with Newton-Nottage have survived and will be referred to in later chapters.

6.

The Tudor and Stuart Periods

By the time the Tudor period began, in 1485, Newton had already developed as a port. This may seem strange to us today because there is only a beach there, but in the fifteenth century a creek ran inland from the sea along the present Beach Road, and was referred to in early documents as 'the Weare at Newton.' The small ships of the day could be drawn up on the banks of the creek when the tide was in, and on the beach itself which was protected against the prevailing westerly wind by the configuration of the coastline. The port became so well known and busy Leland could refer to it in 1538 as 'a Station or Haven for Shippes,' and the trade grew to such an extent that by the end of the seventeenth century records had to be kept, showing that the main exports were wheat, butter, sheep, raw wool and knitted stockings (later coal was added). If a ship or boat came into the creek laden with salt, grain, apples or pears (the main imports) and the cargo sold, a due of one bushel of the produce had to be paid to the lord of the (Pembroke) Manor and even if 'a bark' touched the ground within the creek 'Pillidge' had to be paid. We know that in 1664 a dozen boats plied this trade, manned by sixteen sailors varying in age between 12 and 64, and that their ports of call were on the other side of the channel, principally Bristol and Minehead. Some of the sailors were also farmers, renting fields in the parish, and one, William Leyson, who sailed a craft called 'The Five Brothers of Newton', became quite wealthy, being taxed in 1671 as owning two hearths in his house—very unusual in those days for a commoner.

The same William Leyson, together with his brothers and other sailors connected with the port, showed further enterprise when they leased from the lord of the manor (for a period of ninety nine years) land on which was built 'the mansion called the Weare House.' There is no doubt that this was the building that eventually became known as The Old Red House, and is thought to have been Leyson's home and the headquarters of the traders. Later it became a residence for well-to-do people requiring a bathing holiday, run by Thomas Marment of Pyle. Unfortunately, being only fifty yards from the beach, it became a sand-blown ruin, and no trace of it remains today.

Whilst all this activity was going on at Newton, Nottage was developing into a community devoted to arable farming. Already the land around the village was renowned for agriculture, as is shown by the fact that a grange belonging to the monks of Margam Abbey, called Noge Court, had been set up there. In 1509 this land was leased by the Abbot to Lewis ap Thomas ap Howell and his son, Jankyn, and as part of the dissolved monastery it was later sold to Sir Rice Mansell. We do not know the extent of the estate, but tradition, as well as Thomas Gray (who wrote 'The Buried City of Kenfig') has it that it was land around the present Nottage Court. The Lougher family eventually acquired the property and the house was rebuilt in the Elizabethan style in the middle of the sixteenth century, being given the name Tŷ Mawr (Great House). In 1855 it was renamed Nottage Court by the Rev. H. Hey Knight, who owned it then.

Another house rebuilt at this time in the Elizabethan style was the manor of Sker. Much of the land in this area was also originally in the hands of monks— in this case the monks of Neath Abbey; but in 1536 the Abbot leased the estate to Gwenllian Lougher (widow) for ninety nine years, and after the dissolution of the monasteries it eventually became the property of the Turbervilles of Penlline who, still remaining Catholic after the Restoration, built a priest's hole in the thick walls. For many years Sker House became the secret meeting place of local Catholics, who held services there. Later it became the residence of a long line of gentlemen tenant farmers, one of whom was Isaac Williams, the father of Elizabeth, the famed Maid of Sker, who was courted by Thomas Evans, the carpenter-harpist of Newton—a story not to be confused with R. D. Blackmore's fictitious work 'The Maid of Sker.' Gaunt and eerie, 'a sad and lonesome place, with many gables and chimneys,' as Blackmore described it, the house became the centre of several ghostly legends, including that of the spectre of a monk who came to an untimely end when he lived in the original grange. Sadly the house has been so beaten by storms it has become a ruin.

Between these two great houses much of the land was ideal for farming. As Leland said in 1538, 'there is good Corne and Gresse but little Wood'—not surprising when we remember that few trees of any size can be grown in the Porthcawl area even today because of the prevailing wind. There was also the problem of wind-blown sand that had already put paid to Kenfig, and so serious did this menace become a Commissioner of Sewers was appointed in 1553 with the special responsibility of trying to 'withstand and avoid the rages of the sea.' In the main, however, the fields were rich in soil, allowing good

8 An early engraving of Sker House

husbandry, with grazing for cattle and sheep on three commons. For farmers in Nottage there was the area called 'the Locks', for Newtonians 'the Backs' (between the village and the future Porthcawl) and for both villages, Newton Down, the land on top of the Tŷ Coch and Dan-y-Graig ridges.

Tithe items in the *Valor Ecclesiasticus* of 1535 show that, taken as a whole, Newton-Nottage was in the top league as far as farm produce was concerned. The tenant farmers, who paid their rents at May and Michaelmas, seem to have devoted most of their work to the growing of grain crops, the raising of sheep and the production of wool, with less emphasis on the keeping of cattle. By 1630 there were fifty tenants and sub-tenants and the total of arable land was just under 500 acres, but most of these were in the hands of the land-owners, so the average holding was ten acres or less—not enough to make the tenants wealthy unless they had another source of income like that of the mariner-farmers of Newton. And there was also taxation. In 1523 not only land was taxed but all personal possessions except clothes. This meant that each person had to be assessed (a great annoyance) and the information stored in what are known as Lay Subsidy Rolls. These documents show that in 1524 there were 64 people paying tax in the parish, and a study of the amounts involved reveal what one might expect: that most of the wealth was in the hands of the landed gentry and that the majority of the inhabitants had very little property.

Another irritant to the villagers was that they had to serve on a jury every three weeks, even during the time of harvests. They also had to obey the steward who, appointed by the lord, presided over the courts (sometimes held in the church), and any tenant found guilty of a felony forfeited his goods. The lord also held two Leet or Law Courts within every year—a sort of early police court. Another person not always liked by the villagers was the parson (annual stipend £80), appointed in turn by the three lords of the manor. One, by the name of Thomas Hilliard, who was appointed to the Rectory of Newton-Nottage in 1655, became so unpopular he had difficulty collecting the tithes—an additional burden on top of the taxes. It is interesting to know, too, that at this time the three lords of the manor collected a rent of three shillings a year from the chapel at Nottage, dividing this sum between them.

Towards the end of the Stuart period the population had increased to 82, the tenants holding parcels of land sometimes widely separated—a result of their once having been strips in open fields. By this time the lanes connecting the fields and dwellings had been developed roughly into the pattern that exists today, with West Road, Moor Lane (leading to New Park farm, then owned

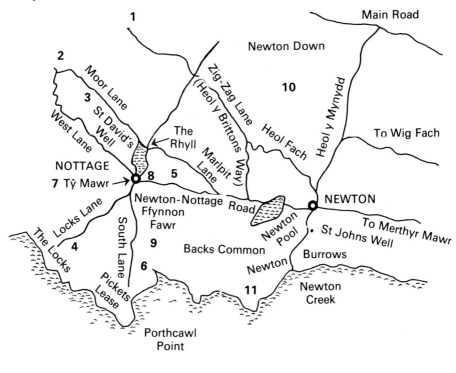

1. Grove
2. New park
3. Mŵr (moor)
4. Hutchwns
5. Shortlands
6. South
7. Tŷ Mawr (Nottage Court)
8. Tŷ Talbot
9. & 10. Windmills
11. Old Red House

9 Sketch map showing early lanes and farms

by Robert Jenkins), Ty'n-y-Caeau, Marlpit Lane and Zig-Zag Lane (Heol-y-Britton's Way) being prominent. Also prominent was Newton-Nottage Road, then much wider in parts than it is now, this being attributed to the fact that Sutton stone was carried in ox carts along its route from quarries in Ogmore to Margam, where it was used in the construction of the monastery. In addition there was an embryo South Road (called 'South' because it ran from the more populated Nottage to a few dwellings near an inlet on the coast), and it is worth remembering that one of today's main thoroughfares, New Road, did not then exist, coming into being only when Porthcawl developed as a dock. The Rhyll, however, was very prominent, being described as a lake—probably because this was a period of increased rainfall. Large, too, was Newton Waun (Newton Pool) and the wetlands around The Wilderness.

One of the principal aims of the Tudors was to guard their new domains against possible enemies, such as Spain, and so they inaugurated what are known as Muster Rolls, which tabulated the number of men who could be called upon in an emergency. The Muster Roll for the Hundred of Newcastle, which included Newton-Nottage, shows that in 1578 (only ten years before the Armada set sail) there were sixty fit men in the area, of whom fifty were equipped but only ten trained and four mounted. They were on an hour's call.

By the second half of the seventeenth century the amount of tenanted land in the three manors had increased to 1000 acres, but the rents were still the same as they had been a hundred years before (no inflation then). The principal landowners were still the lords, the most important being Richard Lougher (the last of the Tythegston and Newton Loughers), Barbara Lougher and Christopher Turberville of Sker. The enterprising Leyson family were still doing well for themselves, acquiring parcels of land all over the place and also renting Pickets (Pickeds) Lease, roughly the sandy area on which modern Porthcawl is built.

Like their Tudor predecessors the Stuart monarchs were also always casting about to find means of increasing their revenue, and this time their officials hit upon the idea of a Hearth Tax, introduced between 1662 and 1689. Between these years records show that there were 83 heads of households in the parish, assessed as having 131 hearths (63 in Nottage and 68 in Newton). Unfortunately this tax does not give us enough information to estimate the total population at that time, especially as ordinary people then began building their cottages without hearths; and to do that we must turn to the Poll Tax, which was brought in on 15th June 1689 to supersede the Hearth Tax. This new tax, payable by all except the poorest people, again meant assessing everybody, making it a greatly disliked tax. This time, however, the tax returns are a great help to us today, for they show that in the last years of the seventeenth century there were 188 adults in the parish, of whom 92 were men. Of the men 38 were tenants, 36 labourers, 14 farm servants (who were paid between £1 and £3 a year) and 4 paupers. Of the 38 tenants 27 were married, the couples having only 48 children between them, so the idea of large families in those days is false. This was probably due to high infant mortality. Taking these figures into account, and comparing them with the returns from other parishes, it becomes possible to assess the total population of Newton-Nottage at the turn of the century. Including people like casual labourers, children of paupers, etc., there were just under three hundred people altogether, a third being men, a third women and a third children.

Yet another tax was introduced before the end of the seventeenth century. This was the Window Tax, and gives us an insight into the number of dwelling houses in the parish. The tax was levied at a rate varying between two shillings (10p) for houses with less than ten windows to ten shillings (50p) for those with more than twenty. Returns show that there were 37 houses with windows, the two buildings having the most windows being Tŷ Mawr (Nottage Court) and Sker House. The redoubtable William Leyson had more than ten windows in the Old Red House and, also high on the list, was Clevis House, referred to as 'a house, garden and orchard called the new house upon the Clieves.'

Probate documents of the seventeenth century are also interesting. These show that the majority of people had little to leave in their wills, the usual things bequeathed being 'wearing apparel' and 'household stuff', with very little money being mentioned. The most expensive items handed down seem to have been feather beds and bedclothes, articles of furniture apparently being judged as having little value. Of ordinary people only the farmer-mariners of Newton seem to have had much to leave, and once more William Leyson must be referred to. He left thirteen acres of land (with its corn) animals and sheep valued at £100 (a considerable sum then), 'parcels of salt and iron' worth £80 and two boats to the total value of £230. His carefully-kept books showed that on his death he owed £180 but that there was £150 due to him.

Although there were footpads and robbers aplenty lying in wait for unwary travellers, the parishioners appear to have been, on the whole, a law abiding lot. Their most heinous offence seems to have been the cutting of sedges, which they used on their hearths and sometimes to roof their homes. Understandably the three lords of the manors took a very serious view of this, for the removal of turf and grass allowed the ever-present sand to make inroads on the arable land, and a survey of the seventeenth century speaks of many cottages 'ruined by the sandes.' The parishioners' betters were not always so well behaved, for some of the young 'blades' of the local gentry seem to have enjoyed forming large gangs of thugs (especially during the Elizabethan era) who frequently indulged in pitched battles. One leader of such a gang, a Turberville of Sker, even made himself known as far as London, where he had to appear before the famed Star Chamber on charges of riotous behaviour. The taxes and privations of ordinary people did not prevent them from being loyal to the Crown, however. A beacon was always kept at the ready on Newton Down in case an enemy appeared, and when the Great Civil War broke out the inhabitants, along with the rest of Wales, declared for the King. The Restoration did not stop the growth of Puritanism in the area, for already by 1660 Nottage had become a meeting place for Calvinistic Baptists. The growth of religious bodies within the parish boundary will be dealt with in a later chapter.

7.

The Eighteenth Century

The lane or 'way' leading from Nottage to the coast has already been mentioned. This track ended near a small inlet sheltered to some degree from westerly gales by a rocky promontory called Porth Cawl Point (also referred to as Porth-y-Cawl). 'Porth' is Welsh for port or gateway and 'Cawl' means broth, so it seems safe to assume that the name is a poetic reference to the appearance of the sea at this place, where it is nearly always being churned into a frothy mass by the prevailing wind. Later, a seventeenth century survey refers to a place called 'Port Call', which can only be an English version of the Welsh name, for there was certainly no port there at that time, all the seafaring activity being centred on Newton. It therefore seems equally safe to assume that the Welsh form came first, the two words being eventually placed in juxtaposition to form Porthcawl. Because neither the town nor the dock was created until the nineteenth century an account of their development must wait until later. In the meantime Nottage and Newton were carrying on much as they had done for the last two hundred years.

Changes were taking place however. Although in 1700 the three manors were still in the possession of their original owners, within thirty years the

10   Nottage Court, originally called Tŷ Mawr

Lougher Manor with Tythegston had passed by marriage to Robert Knight of Bristol; and his son, Henry, then purchased the Pembroke Manor. This substantial amalgamation of two estates within one family was further enhanced by the subtle purchasing of land within the parish boundary, transactions masterminded by Henry Knight's aunt, Anne Basset. For a while, therefore, the Knight family became the principal landowners in Newton-Nottage, and one of the purchases was Tŷ Mawr, subsequently re-named Nottage Court. Two Knights, Robert and Henry Hey, later became Rectors of the parish. In the meantime the male line of the Herbert family had become extinct and the estate passed to Calvert Richard Jones and Herbert Hurst.

Much of the land was leased in the eighteenth century to tenant farmers. Hutchwn's farm (spelled Hudgeon in old maps and now remembered only by the name Hutchwn's Close) consisted of a house and 11½ acres of land worked by William Saphin. Two farms called South, lying astride South Lane, were held by Richard Cradock (a family name well known in the parish since Norman times) and Morgan Harry. Land at Grove, originally owned by the Loughers, was leased to a Richard Thomas. At first this farm was called Burdon's Grove, after the family who worked it in the fourteenth century, and the lane leading to it known as Burdon's Way—later corrupted to Heol-y-Britton's Way. In 1768 there was a sub-tenant in occupation called William Turpin—no relation of the notorious highwayman. Tŷ Talbot (once owned by Lord Talbot, hence the name) then consisted of two houses, outbuildings and 79 acres of land, leased to Richard Burnell, yeoman. New Park farm, originally one of the closes of Sker Grange when it was owned by the monks of Neath Abbey, was still in the hands of the Turbervilles. A house and 26 acres at Mŵr (in Moor lane) was leased in 1742 to a Mary Jenkins at an annual rent of £5, but she also had to pay 1s 6d (7½p) in lieu of work at the lord's corn harvest and 'two fat hens every Christmas.' An old map shows that Shortlands was also a self-contained farm at this time on Tŷ Mawr land, itself consisting of 155 acres. Old West farm and West farm (originally Tŷ Coroner) were worked by tenants living in Nottage. Top farm (the farmhouse is now Veronica Cottage) was tenanted by Watkin Leyson before being taken over by the Knight family, and there were also West End farm (known today as Tudor Cottage) and Home farm, near the present Farmers' Arms public house. Labourers to work the land of all these farms were hired every May Day at a wall abutting the village green—appropriately called Labourers' Wall—and to grind the increasing yield of corn a second windmill (the first was on Newton Down) was built on South Road.

In the eighteenth century a land tax was reintroduced, payable by all occupiers (tenants as well as owners). The rate varied from 1s (5p) to 4s. (20p) in the pound according to whether the country was at war or not—a frequent occurrence in those days—and each parish was assessed on the total amount by the central government. Thus in 1724 the parish had to pay over £33 but in 1795 (during the war against France) it had gone up to £80—two and a half times as much. In addition each parish had to levy rates to pay for such things as alms to the poor. So in the eighteenth century the method familiar to us today by which central and local governments raised money (rates and taxes) was already in being. Then, as now, people grumbled but had to pay up. It is interesting to know that the rateable value of Newton-Nottage in 1750 was just over £300.

Also interesting are the church records of the last half of the eighteenth century. These show that the average number of baptisms in the parish was nine per annum, although this is not a true picture of the birth rate for illegitimate children were not recorded. The average annual number of burials was just under seven, and there were only about three marriages a year, mostly among local people, showing that there was still only limited movement by the population. Towards the end of the century the following people, listed by occupation, got married in the church: 1 Rector (the Rev. Robert Davies, who became the Lord of Pembroke Manor and also Rector of Newton-Nottage in 1743), 1 lawyer (William H. Jones), 1 surgeon (Thomas Bennet), 1 school-master, 5 yeomen, 4 blacksmiths, 1 carpenter, 1 clockmaker, 1 cooper, 8 shoemakers, 1 miner, 2 tailors, 1 tanner and 2 weavers. Burial tombs inside and outside the church are inscribed with names that had become synonymous with the growth of the parish since its earliest days, such as Lougher, Knight, Cradock, Nowell and Leyson. Also buried there is Edward Thomas, Clerk to the Parish, and four generations of his descendants who have filled that office. Mariners who had drowned on the treacherous coast were buried usually along the south wall of the churchyard.

As the century drew to a close the 'Weare House of Newton', later re-named 'The Old Red House', was converted into an hotel for 'Gentry requiring a sea-bathing holiday', an amenity advertised in the newspapers of the day. One of the guests was Dr Richard Price, and it is said that Josiah Wedgwood, after a stay there, obtained inspiration for his china colours from the pebbles he found lying on the beach. Nottage, not to be out-done, was also becoming prominent through the activity of its tenant-farmers. The Glamorgan Agricultural Society Show, begun in 1772, saw much of the local yeomen's produce, no doubt as a result of the new methods in agriculture being introduced then. This was also the time of the acceleration of Enclosures, when land-owners were grouping the old strips and smaller fields into larger ones, thus doing away with much waste and aiding innovations. In the country as a whole the enclosing of land, especially when it involved common land, certainly resulted in 'fat beasts and thin men' but there is no evidence that this movement caused a great deal of distress in the parish in the eighteenth century. This is probably because the tenanted land in the area was already quite substantial and being successfully farmed by yeomen. In the next century this was to change, for then enclosures of common land deprived smaller tenants of many of their grazing rights, causing considerable suffering.

There was, however, a more sinister side to the villagers' activities. The sailors of Newton had long been aware that their coastline was one of the most dangerous in the country, with vicious traps for unwary mariners. To the east were the precipitous cliffs of Dunraven and Nash, to the south and west jagged reefs called the Black Rocks and the Tuskars, and just off Sker the treacherous shifting sands known as the Scarweathers. Many a ship had been wrecked on these places, but now, because of increased trade, merchant-men were bigger and contained much valuable cargo. It is not thought that the villagers indulged in deliberate wrecking such as occurred further up the coast (Wick, Dunraven and Nash were reputed to be the haunts of the wrecking gangs) but there is no doubt that Newtonians never looked a gift horse in the mouth. If a wreck occurred they plundered it. Not only was the cargo taken but every nail and plank in the ship soon disappeared. Sometimes their greed became too great, as in 1770 when the 'Planter's Welvard' ran aground on Newton Beach. This was a Dutch vessel of 770 tons bound for Amsterdam and carrying a cargo of sugar, coffee, cocoa and cotton. The beach was strewn with merchandise, fast disappearing into the homes of the villagers—so fast that a Customs Official was sent to stop the pillaging. He managed to seize eight horses laden with coffee but could do little else. He wrote, 'We have given a constant attendance there at great expense to stop the cargo being embezzled by the Country people and to use our endeavours to save the ship, but fear we shall do neither as the Country people are quite outrageous and threaten our lives.' The three sons of a J. S. Jackert, who were on their way to Holland to be educated, lost their lives in the wreck and were buried in Newton churchyard.

Mention has already been made of the fact that ordinary people travelled very infrequently outside the parish boundaries in those days. This was not only because they had little spare money but also because the eighteenth-century highways were exceedingly unsafe, especially for those travelling on foot. The main road out of the area, called Heol-y-Mynydd, ran from Newton to the coaching road (the present A48) at Red Hill, where there was a toll gate— another impediment to free movement. If a traveller went westward there was the danger that he might be set upon by the Cefn Riders. No information has been found to substantiate the existence of these robbers, but legends connected with them are so numerous and persistent there seems little doubt that they did terrorise the region in those days, their apparent speciality being robbing farms in wide, sweeping raids. If the traveller went eastward there was the menace of numerous footpads who infested the approaches to Bridgend and Ogmore; and for coaches which ran between Swansea and Cardiff (with connections for London and Bristol) the most dreaded part of the road was Crack Hill, where the horses were slowed by the gradient. Both robbers and the Devil himself were said to reside there. Nor could the traveller always find safety in the coaching inns, as the story of Cap Coch shows. A Bridgend man, whose real name was Twch, he had the foresight to build an hostelry called the New Inn only a few yards away from the Merthyr Mawr dipping bridge at Ewenny, which then lay on the main coaching road. Wearing a red cap (hence the name) only when he went on one of his frequent smuggling trips to Revolutionary France, he added to his income by murdering travellers who stayed at the inn, later selling their possessions in Bridgend market. He was eventually hanged on

Stalling Down, near Cowbridge, on a charge of stealing a sheep, and after his death scores of bodies were found buried in and around the New Inn.

One of the most lucrative occupations in the eighteenth century was smuggling. There is little doubt that the mariners of Newton took part in this activity, not only bringing in goods from the continent but also merchandise from across the Bristol Channel to avoid paying dues to the lord of the manor; and stories handed down suggest that a tavern and brew-house on the site of the present Jolly Sailor became the smugglers' headquarters. All this danger did not stop the wealthy from travelling, however, for they had the money to arm themselves with pistols, and a special gun was devised to ensure their safety if they travelled by coach—the blunderbuss.

By the time the eighteenth century was coming to an end, Newton and Nottage had become substantial villages whose populations had been steadily increasing over the last hundred years. The number of people in Newton had risen to 254, living in 55 houses, and Nottage had 217 inhabitants in 43 houses. Although Nottage was the smaller it was more important agriculturally, having most of the farming land in its vicinity, and its tenant farmers were still winning prizes in the Glamorgan Agricultural Society. Probably because it lay nearer the ever-encroaching sand Newton was not so well blessed with agricultural land, and so its inhabitants were engaged in other occupations as, for example, the sailors who were still keeping the creek active. Soon, however, both villages were to be eclipsed by the building of docks and a town near the promontory Porth Cawl Point.

8.

The Porthcawl Docks

When the nineteenth century began the area around the future town of Porthcawl was much the same as it had been for the previous two hundred years. The two villages of Newton and Nottage, together with a few scattered farmsteads, were connected by a system of lanes and 'ways' which we would recognise today, with the enclosed agricultural land lying mainly to the north and west of the present New Road. A stream still ran from The Rhyll to the sea at Sandy Bay, passing through pools and wetlands much larger in size than they are today. There were three commons (Locks, Backs and Newton Down) and several sandy acres called Pickets Lease, on which much of the future town was to be built. The Lougher and Pembroke Manors were held by Colonel Knight of Tythegston, and when he died the Lougher estate passed to his oldest nephew, the Rev. Robert Knight, and the Pembroke Manor eventually to a younger nephew, the Rev. Henry Hey Knight. Later the Lougher estates were sold to Sir Josiah Guest, and so the three manors once again reverted to different owners.

Against this rural background events were taking place to the north and west of the parish boundary. In the Llynfi and Cefn areas minerals (including coal) had already been discovered and were being extracted. The problem was how to distribute these minerals to lucrative markets, so in 1818 a group of men investigated the possibility of providing an outlet for the new-found wealth. They met at the Globe Inn, in Bridgend, to consider 'the possibility of making a safe and sufficient harbour' at the mouth of the Ogmore River, but the water there was too turbulent and in any case the landowner was afraid that a dock would despoil his estate. The scheme was therefore abandoned. Next they looked at Newton, where there was already a well-established 'port', but the topography of the hinterland meant that the construction of a tramroad would be prohibitively expensive. Not to be beaten they inspected, and decided on, a site in the lee of a small promontory called Porth Cawl Point—also referred to as Pwll (Pool) Cawl Point.

The interested parties met in January 1825 at the Wyndham Arms Inn, Bridgend, and there were many illustrious names in the group: the Earl of Dunraven, Sir John Nicholl, M.P., Mr Talbot, Major Mackworth, Colonel Knight, the Rev. Robert Knight and Messrs. Guest, Crawshay, Coffin and Buckland. They applied for, and obtained, an Act of Parliament to authorise the construction of a tramroad and the improvement of 'the port of Pwll Cawl.' The Act was passed that same year and the shareholders of the new undertaking met (again at the Wyndham Arms) to plan operations. The objective was to build the tramroad 'from a place called Dyffryn Llynfi in the parish of Llangynwyd to a bay called Pwll Cawl, otherwise Porth Cawl in the parish of Newton-Nottage' and to the improving of the bay by the erection of a jetty. The estimated cost of £40,000 had already been subscribed in £100 shares by 57 people, and authority was obtained to raise another £20,000 on mortgage 'should it be required.' At first all the principal shareholders were men residing in South Wales, but later many others outside the area joined in (including Benjamin Disraeli to the tune of £3,000).

The tramroad was planned by J. Hodgkinson of Newport. Begun in 1825 it was ready for horse-drawn traffic three years later. Meanwhile a small tidal basin was constructed at the sea end. Originally it was a rectangle enclosed by four walls, the huge blocks being fashioned out of local stone, with a gap in the eastern side for ships to enter and leave. (The gap was later filled in but its outline can still be seen today.)

The new Duffryn, Llynvi and Porthcawl Railway Company (the anglicised spelling was used in the Act) got off to a shaky start, however, for the small dock was tidal and open to fierce gales, and the first attempt at a breakwater, being just a stumpy addition to the promontory, was not big enough to give adequate shelter to the harbour entrance. Quickly the company ran out of

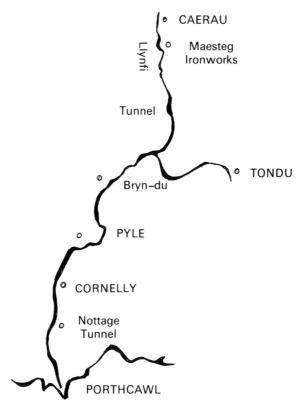

11 Route of old tramroad

funds, and so another Act of Parliament had to be passed allowing the additional raising of money. In spite of further expenditure on the dock its open aspect continued to make it difficult for ships to berth and leave in the winter months, and even after 1832, when the two lighthouses at Nash Point had been constructed (transom lights to aid navigation) the port was still used mainly in the summer only. The result of all this was that when the first dividend was declared it was only one per cent.

The inadequacy of the dock became more apparent in 1833 when the Maesteg ironworks, the Coegnant Spelter works and the furnaces at Bryn-du were becoming busy. There were also collieries starting up along the line of the tramroad, and when the Cambrian Ironworks in the Llynfi valley and the Tondu Ironworks came on stream something had to be done. The result was yet another Act (in 1840) authorising the raising of further capital, and the money was put to good use. New facilities (ramps and chutes) were constructed to speed up the loading of coal and the dock was enlarged by extending the basin fifty yards to the north. These measures resulted in an increased use of the port, so much so that after paying the interest on the mortgage the dividend

41

leaped to 8%. Trade continued to increase, with the trams making five regular journeys every day (each journey took six hours) and in 1845 records show that over 35,000 tons of coal and 21,000 tons of iron were exported. The regular half-yearly dividend settled down around the 3½ to 4 per cent mark.

By this time the railway mania had started in Britain, encouraging the Company to convert the horse-drawn tramline into a steam engine railway. Again a meeting of shareholders was held at the Wyndham Arms (in September 1845) but little came of it. However, a year later the Llynvi Valley Railway Company was formed and in 1847 it took over the Duffryn, Llynvi and Porthcawl Railway Company. It looked as though the dock would now obtain a greatly increased trade, but unfortunately a recession developed in the iron industry. Nevertheless a broad-gauge steam engine railway was constructed to run from Maesteg to a junction with the main South Wales line at Bridgend. At the same time broad-gauge rails were laid to replace the tramroad from Tondu to Porthcawl.

This was the position when a new driving force came on the scene—the Brogdens. A family firm based in Sale, Manchester, specialising in iron-ore mining and railway construction, John Brogden and Sons had been attracted to South Wales by the mineral wealth then being extracted in large quantities. The firm lost no time in purchasing from Sir Robert Price a controlling interest in the Tondu Ironworks, and within a few years had started mining for coal in the Ogmore Valley, which was being served by the Ogmore Valley Railway Company. At the instigation of the Brogdens this company built a standard-guage railway from Nantymoel to Tondu and then extended the line to Porthcawl. When this railway opened in August 1865 the Porthcawl Dock became the terminus for all the steam-driven freight trains from both the Llynfi and Ogmore Valleys.

The Brogdens were also instrumental in obtaining an Act of Parliament authorising a huge development in the dock and James Brogden, the younger son and partner, was put in charge of the undertaking. First a much larger dock (the inner harbour) was constructed with an entrance and gates in the north wall of the old basin. Then the latter's eastern entrance (the one facing Sandy Bay) was blocked up and a new one created in its southern wall. To protect the new entrance a massive breakwater was built, extending the old and inadequate defence wall by over 100 yards. This gave the new complex a much greater degree of protection against westerly gales. Finally a wooden jetty was erected at the apex of the old dock's retaining wall and new coal chutes and railway sidings installed along the western wharf of the inner harbour. All this work was completed at a cost of a quarter of a million pounds and opened amidst general rejoicing in July 1867. A new steamer of 547 tons, named 'The John Brogden' in honour of the head of the firm, was prominent at the ceremony.

The new dock prospered immediately, so much so that in 1871 it shipped over 165,000 tons of coal and iron; and when the Great Western Railway Company took over the Llynvi and Ogmore Railway Company two years later it was able to guarantee shareholders a dividend of 6%, an optimism that

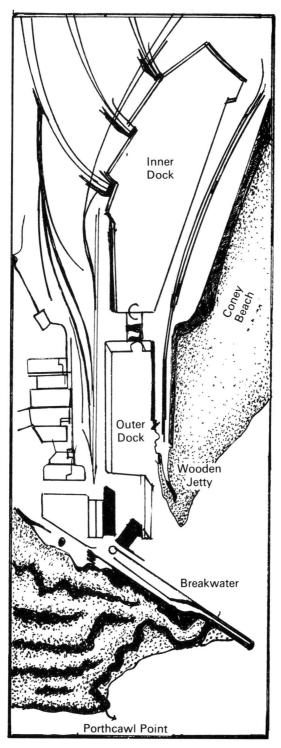

Inner
Dock

Coney
Beach

Outer
Dock

Wooden
Jetty

Breakwater

Porthcawl Point

12 Porthcawl docks

13   North end of the dock in 1890

seemed justified by further progress. In 1874, for example, more than 700 vessels were using the port. Admittedly most of these were small sailing ships of under 100 tons engaged in coastal trade, but some were quite large taking cargoes as far afield as Valparaiso. For the far-seeing, however, there were danger signals ahead. More than half the returning vessels brought in cargoes and had to be filled with profitless ballast, usually in the form of rocks which were off-loaded and dumped on a ballast tip—then the rabbit infested warren we know today as the fairground. The cargoes that were brought in consisted mainly of iron ore and pit-props for the collieries that lined the railroad, but the real danger lay in the fact that ninety per cent of the out-going freight was coal only—a dependence on one commodity which was eventually to prove fatal.

The first blow came when the Bessemer process was introduced. The importation of a much purer iron ore from Spain caused many of the South Wales iron works to close down or move to the coast. The Brogdens, whose undertakings now provided two thirds of the outgoing cargoes from Porthcawl, were badly hit. They tried desperately to form a new company, the Llynfi, Tondu and Ogmore Iron and Coal Company, but this, too, began to founder and an Official Receiver was appointed in 1880. All the Brogden enterprises were taken over by the North's Navigation Collieries Company, and at first this seems to have been a successful business arrangement, for trade at the dock revived. In 1892 the number of vessels that used the port had risen to 800 (some of them over 1,000 tons) and now half of them were steam-powered. In that year a record 227,000 tons of coal was exported from the wharves. All seemed set for a prosperous future. But the Achilles' Heel was still there: the over-dependence on one main commodity, coal; and still three-quarters of the ships came in light or laden with ballast. These weaknesses, added to by other factors that had been apparent from the beginning, namely tidal docking, an exposed position in spite of the new breakwater and the ever-present danger of reefs and sand shoals, meant that ultimate demise was certain. The final blow came in 1892 when two large docks opened at Port Talbot and Barry. These docks could be used at all times, irrespective of tides, and the former was an ideal outlet for the coal of the Llynfi, Ogmore and Garw Valleys. Porthcawl could not compete, for it was impossible to extend the docks inland (it would still have been tidal even if this could have been done) and within a year of Port Talbot starting up the shipment of coal from Porthcawl dropped to one-eighth of its normal annual amount.

In 1901 an attempt was made to improve the trade, and a committee was formed to consider how this could be done, but to no avail. Port Talbot and Barry docks prospered but Porthcawl continued to decline. All but one of the ramps and chutes were dismantled, and in 1903 only 2,700 tons of coal were exported. The final closure came in 1906. A few small ships still came in carrying such things as bricks from Bridgwater and timber for Jenning's yard— to be used in building the now rapidly developing town. Under a Great Western Railway Company Act of 1913 the outer basin, the breakwater and the Cosy Corner site (so named because a comfortable cinema was later built there by the Beynon family) were handed over to the Porthcawl Urban District Council. The company began filling in the inner dock but when World War I broke out this work was discontinued, and for a time after the war the harbour facilities were used for the breaking up of captured German vessels. The final filling in of the dock went on during and after World War II and became a huge and unsightly car park. Porthcawl had ended its short and vacillating career as a port. The town that had grown around the dock went on expanding, however, and although its inhabitants did not then realise it, Porthcawl was poised to begin another phase in its development: that of a major seaside holiday resort.

9.

Porthcawl: Early Development

Before the first small dock came into being there were few buildings outside the boundaries of Newton and Nottage. Farms such as Grove, New Park, Mŵr, Hutchwns, South and Shortlands (then on Tŷ Mawr land and called Hen Dŷ) had long existed, and there were two windmills, one at South Road and the other on Newton Down. The latter was let to a miller on condition that he freely ground corn for the Lord of the Manor, and one of its earlier tenants was William Weston Young, of whom more later. The Weare House at Newton (now called Tŷ Coch—Red House) was still standing and there was a cabin near Porth Cawl Point owned by Colonel Henry Knight. In the nineteenth century other farms were brought into being such as Tŷ Coch and Morfa (the latter created from Tŷ Mawr land when it became a private residence). Two other farms, Mount Pleasant and Dan-y-Lan (later named Coed-ar-Graig) were the direct result of the Enclosure movement. Rock House in South Road had been built as had Dan-y-Graig House (about 1817 by the Rev. Robert Knight), but the over-all picture was still one of two separate villages and a few scattered homesteads.

All this was to change with the arrival of the tramroad. The workers on this and the dock required living accommodation, and so buildings sprang up near the harbour, on Pickets Lease and at the southern end of South Road. Amongst the earliest structures was a house on the site of the present Knight's Arms (with a shop next door), a building which eventually became the General Picton and the large cottage in Esplanade Avenue, built by the mariner Peter Lewis. John Elias built a cottage which was the fore-runner of similar dwellings called Lias Cottages (the cottages and Lias Road were named after him and not the limestone rock), and a steam saw-mill was erected at the bottom of the present Station Hill.

By 1845 the dock was prospering, drawing in more workers, and so the number of buildings increased rapidly. Warehouses and store-yards were constructed near the wharves and a row of cottages appeared nearby. Originally called Company Row it became known as Pilot Row (now the site of the Pier Hotel). Other cottages were built near the tramroad, around the steam mill, along South Road and for the first time buildings appeared on an embryo New Road. Philadelphia Road was begun about 1847 and housed many of the steadily increasing population. To cater for the thirst of the new army of workers' public houses sprang up everywhere, the majority of them being rapidly converted private houses and cottages. The earliest were the Knight's Arms, the General Picton, the Three Horse Shoes, the Ship and Castle and the Harbour Inn (subsequently Ye Pirates' Club). There was also the Ship Aground (near the docks) and the Star Inn (on South Road). Even Colonel Knight's cottage was pressed into service, becoming the Anchor public house (later the Anchor Cafe) and there was a beer house called the Royal Oak. As more dock workers came into the area a second generation of inns appeared: the Brogden, the Victoria Inn, the Queen's Hotel, the Greyhound and the Mason's Arms. (A fuller account of these establishments is given later in the section 'Inns and Public Houses'.)

By now (the middle of the nineteenth century) the budding new town, already being referred to by its present name, Porthcawl, had a population slightly greater than that of either Newton or Nottage. Indeed Newton, in spite of possessing two pleasant inns called the Crown (which was also a small brewery and is now a private house) and the Ancient Briton (later renamed the Newton Hotel before reverting to its old name) was described by a traveller as being 'a decayed bathing village', and the same writer dismissed Nottage as being nothing more than 'a cluster of farm houses and cottages.' The importance of the new industrial area is shown by the fact that in 1850 it had a post office (on the site of the present Sidoli' Cafe, opposite Woolworths) a constable, a harbour-master and two officially appointed overseers. There were also several shops (including four greengrocers), two private schools and a mission church for Wesleyans on the dockside (they were soon to move to their present site). Horse-drawn carriages ran to either Pyle or Red Hill to make connections with the Royal Mail coaches which ran daily and a packet boat left for Bristol every eighth day. In the eighteen-sixties development went on apace. New Road was constructed to link Porthcawl with Newton and houses went up along parts of its sandy surface. Two of the cottages were taken over by Dr James Lewis of Maesteg and became known as 'The Rest'—later 'The Old Rest' when Dr Lewis built the new Convalescent Home at Rest Bay. Also constructed at this time was Hookland Road, intended at its inception to connect the main thoroughfare with Newton-Nottage Road.

All this was haphazard development, however, for there was no real master plan. The dock went on working, the tramway continued to bring freight from the valleys, but dwellings and public houses went up often in isolation from each other. It required the genius of one man to put things in order, and that man was James Brogden, who had already master-minded the creation of the new dock. Even while working on that task his fertile mind had been formulating various schemes, and when the opportunity came to develop a large town as well he could not resist the challenge. Unfortunately, as we shall see, his first attempt was short-lived.

10.

The Town of Porthcawl

After sketching out rough drafts of the town he proposed to build James Brogden turned to the more practical task of acquiring land. In 1865 he purchased thirty acres of land on Pickets Lease and another area between the present Griffin Park and Mackworth Road. The first thoroughfare to be constructed was given the name John Street in honour of his father, and no time was lost in placing contracts with two builders, George Dement and Joe Lill. The first houses and shops went up where John Street met Well Street (so called because a well had been sunk behind the future Esplanade Hotel) thus forming a nucleus from which it was proposed to expand in all directions. Dement also built a house (called New House) on the site of the present Sea Bank Hotel. Later the place was re-named Sea Bank House and became James Brogden's residence. Being a generous person he also gave the land on which the Wesleyan chapel had been built and willingly exchanged a plot so that the National School could be erected in Lias Road. This fine old building was also used for a time as an Anglican church, but has now been demolished and the site used to build a super-store. In this context it must be mentioned that three other chapels were being constructed at this time: Bethel (built in 1866), Old Gilgal (1869) and the first English Congregational Chapel in New Road (in 1872 where the Masonic temple stands today).

Unfortunately this early attempt to create a town came to an abrupt and unexpected end. John Brogden died in 1869 and his eldest son, Alexander, became the head of the firm, taking up residence at Tondu House, the family mansion. Alexander and James, who had rarely seen eye to eye, quarrelled violently and James, who by this time had been divorced from his wife, Helen, was sent to New Zealand to supervise the construction of a railway. His plans for Porthcawl had to be left in abeyance, with very little accomplished. Building still went on during his absence, however. New dwellings went up along New and South Roads, and those manifestations of a real Victorian town also appeared: a railway station (at the southern end of South Road, first station-master Charles Dalby) and a gas works (near the future Griffin Park). As befitted a growing port there was also a ship-building yard at the northern end of the inner dock and a lifeboat station on the seafront near the present Pier Hotel.

Quite a lot had therefore occurred during James Brogden's absence, but on his return he threw himself into his self-appointed task with all his old vigour, and this time he had two advantages denied to him before. First, the family's industrial undertakings in Mid-Glamorgan having failed, Alexander left the area leaving James a free hand to do as he pleased. Secondly, having become divorced from his first wife, James married (in 1874) Mary Caroline Beete, a relative of General Picton of Waterloo fame (after whom a street and a public house were to be named), and the union was a happy one. Indeed, Mary Caroline not only supported her husband in planning the town but from the beginning she took the lead in arranging many of the innovations that were to come about. The couple took up residence at Sea Bank House and in 1880 Mrs Brogden purchased with her own money the land on Pickets Lease which James had bought for the family firm fifteen years previously, but which had to be given up when the crash came. Additional money for building the projects was obtained by raising mortgages, which were quickly and easily arranged. All was now set for real expansion.

The first project was the building of an esplanade and carriageway along the seafront, complete with a modern hotel and fine terraced houses. Leading off from the esplanade two more streets were planned, both named after Mrs

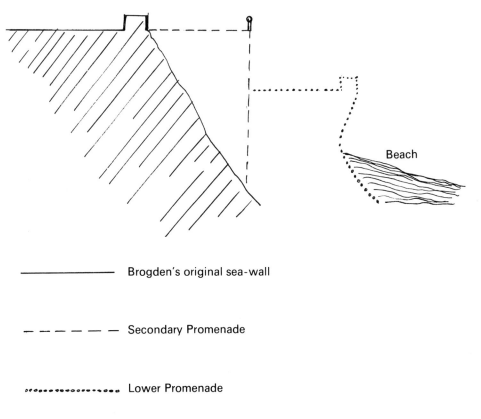

——————————— Brogden's original sea-wall

— — — — — — Secondary Promenade

•••••••••••••••• Lower Promenade

14 The three promenades

Brogden—Mary Street and Caroline Street (the latter was later re-named Esplanade Avenue by R. E. Jones). Building went on along the western side of John Street, both to the north and the south of its junction with Well Street, with a special site for the police station (now the Council Information Centre and the town's Museum), and in 1883 the eastern side of the street was started. One of the buildings here was to become the Porthcawl Hotel, subsequently enlarged to the size it is now. By 1896 John Street was largely completed and a start was made on Railway Terrace (later re-named Hillsborough Place). Twelve houses were erected here and the Terrace linked with John Street by a short thoroughfare called James Street—probably at Mary Brogden's insistence. Well Street was also built up on its southern side.

Whilst this work was going on the esplanade was constructed. Completed in 1887, it consisted of a broad carriageway and an equally broad promenade for pedestrians, replete with seats and an attractive Victorian shelter (subsequently demolished, much to the regret of Porthcawlians). The esplanade ran from the iron gate that guarded the entrance to Locks Common (hence Irongate Point) and ran in a graceful curve towards the slipway in the lee of the breakwater. On it the Marine Hotel and the Esplanade Hotel were built, finished in 1886 and 1887 respectively. Along the carriageway parking spaces were reserved for a dozen or so horse-drawn carriages to cater for the visitors who were already coming to the town in considerable numbers. Guarding the promenade was a sea wall that sloped to the beach at an angle of about forty-five degrees. In normal weather it protected the promenade and its buildings but in stormy conditions the waves could break over the new structures and cascade into John Street and Mary Street, which were sometimes knee-deep in salt water; but this seemed a small price to pay for a burgeoning seaside resort. Those who wish to examine its construction today can do so from the lower promenade at its eastern end.

By 1891 many parts of the parish were illuminated by gas provided by the Porthcawl Gas, Light and Coke Company, situated on land adjacent to the present Griffin Park. The works were kept supplied by coal wagons running on rails which crossed a roadway eventually to be known as the Eastern Promenade. The unguarded crossing caused much consternation among the horse-drawn traffic of the day, a state of affairs that continued well into the twentieth century when motor cars used the route. Many of the new houses were also provided with the luxury of piped water and good pavements. In 1892 the National School in Lias Road had become a place of full-time education for local children, for the Anglican community had erected an iron church in Victoria Avenue and were able to hold their services there until the present stone church was built. A year later Porthcawl, together with the villages of Newton and Nottage, became a Local Government District and in 1894 this elected body became the Porthcawl Urban District Council.

Unfortunately, as has already been related, the trade at the dock was now declining rapidly, the port having been superseded by the bigger tidal outlets at Port Talbot and Barry. In the recession that followed many dock workers and their families moved away and in 1901 there were over a hundred empty houses in the area. Although they tried hard to retrieve the situation, even going to the extent of endeavouring to start a new company, the Brogdens failed to save the port and it was finally closed in 1906. Mrs Brogden, heavily encumbered by mortgages she could not pay off, had to release to the new Urban District Council the promenade which she could no longer maintain. In 1907 James Brogden died, and his wife's mortgagees finally foreclosed. Sea Bank House was sold to John Elias and other men, the area around Mackworth Road to Mr (later Sir) T. G. Jones, and what was left of Pickets Lease went to R. E. Jones. All other parcels of land were taken up by the Lamberts, who then proceeded to develop them along the lines already planned by the Brogdens. The work of this gifted and generous couple had come to an end.

But what they had accomplished has lasted to this day. Although the docks had failed, Porthcawl was now developing as a sea-side resort. For this it was ideally suited, for it had many fine beaches and its crowning glory was the broad promenade. Many hotels—the Esplanade, the Marine, the Porthcawl, as well as Comley's, White's and Evans' Temperance Hotels—were well able to cater for the many holiday-makers and day-trippers who were now coming to the town, their journeys expedited by an excellent railway system. Many Cardiff businessmen also took advantage of the railway to set up home here. The health-giving properties of the bracing air were becoming well-known, too, one of the reasons why the convalescent home was built at Rest Bay. There was even a nine-hole golf course on Locks Common. Started in 1891 the club moved a few years later to its present position just outside the parish boundary. For those whose inclinations were less sporting the town now boasted a variety of excellent shops and, of course, most of the public houses which had been built during the century were still in existence.

Later developers such as the Lamberts and R. E. Jones were to complete the process by which Porthcawl became one of the premier seaside resorts of Wales, but the inspiration and genius that made it all possible belongs to James Brogden and his able and energetic wife. They were both unlucky in that they were unable to benefit from the fruits of their labours, and they paid the penalty of trying to do too much all at once (the later hectic development of the town was compressed into a space of eighteen years) but their plans had been carefully laid, and it was the firm base they provided that made all future development possible.

11.

The Beginning of a Seaside Resort

Land to the north of Pickets Lease which Mrs Brogden had to release went to Lord Wimborne who sold it in 1906 to Harry and John Lambert. They went on developing the site along the lines James Brogden had originally mapped out, and so there came into being Victoria Avenue (as far as Restways), Suffolk Place, Westbourne Place, George Street and Fenton Place, all completed by 1914. Meanwhile R. E. Jones went on building in Mary Street and Caroline Street, the latter being re-named Esplanade Avenue. New Road was extended as far as Queen's Avenue and Mackworth Road, near which the new Board School was opened in 1914. Also in that year the iron church in Victoria Avenue was dismantled and sent to Maesteg where it became a Mission Church, and in its place was built the fine structure known today as All Saints. Water for the new houses came from Craig-yr-Aber, near Margam, to be augmented later by a service reservoir at Tŷ Coch. Sewage went to a pumping station at Mackworth Road, and when the western part of the town was developed an additional outlet to the sea was constructed at Iron Gate Point. By now the combined total population of the parish had increased to 5,000, expanded in the summer months by holiday-makers and day trippers.

In 1914 World War I broke out and after a while further development became desultory. Porthcawl men responded to Kitchener's famous pointing finger and joined the armed forces 'to give the Kaiser a thrashing'. As might be expected of a maritime town many enlisted in the navy and served in the huge fleets which were eventually to bring about the surrender of the German navy at Scapa Flow. Others went into the army, expecting the war to be 'over by Christmas', but the conflict developed into one of stagnating trench warfare, with battles of attrition taking a fearful toll of men's lives. The Government had to cast its net further afield to obtain fresh recruits, and eventually succumbed to the clamour to use men under 5 feet 3 inches in height (previously the Army Council, in its wisdom, had considered that men under that height would not make good soldiers). The result was the formation of the 'Bantam Battalions', so called because all the men, except their officers, were small in stature. Many units were raised in places as far afield as Yorkshire and Canada, and Porthcawl became the training area for one, the 18th Battalion The Welch Regiment. Men flocked to the colours from all over South Wales, including many miners from the valleys who could have remained in a reserved occupation. The Battalion completed its training in Southern England and then moved to France, where it took part in some of the heaviest fighting in the war, suffering a large number of casualties, especially at a place called Mametz Wood. Eventually, after many losses, the Battalions were incorporated into other units, much to the men's chagrin, and so lost their identity. After the war the 18th Battalion's Colours, presented to them by the King, were laid up in All Saints Church, to be kept in the safe keeping of the parish. Over the years the flag began to succumb to the ravages of time, but was skilfully and lovingly restored in 1986 at the instigation of the British Legion, and once more has a place of honour in the church. Also in the grounds of All Saints is the town's cenotaph, which records the names of the 77 men who paid the supreme sacrifice in the four years of warfare.

When the armistice came in 1918 Porthcawl, along with the rest of the country, rejoiced that 'the war to end wars' was finally over but no sooner had the men come home when a trade recession began. The town was able to escape most of the ravages of the 'Great Depression' however, for it was becoming well known as a sea-side resort. This was also the period when the motor car, previously the prerogative of the rich, was being built by mass-production methods, giving a flexibility of movement to many ordinary people. Holiday-makers began to arrive in Porthcawl in their own transport, and the place was also ideal for commuting to such places as Swansea and Cardiff. The town responded to the increased wealth this brought in by continuing to expand.

By 1925 Picton Avenue, Blundell Avenue, Park Avenue, South Road, Lewis Place, Suffolk Place, Arlington Road and South Place had largely been completed, to be followed in the 'thirties by The Green Avenue, Lougher Gardens,

Severn Road, Fairfax Crescent, Northways and Nicholls Avenue. West Road and Newton-Nottage Road were also being extended, with the result that in the inter-war years nearly 1000 houses went up, an average of about fifty a year.

But it was in the providing of amenities that the town began to excel, most of them at the instigation of the Council. Thus the Pavilion (then even more attractive with winter gardens) was opened in August 1932 at a cost of £25,000, becoming the focal centre of the resort and a venue for live entertainment. Within a few years it had also become a much-used conference centre, particularly for the miners of South Wales. The lower promenade was completed in 1935 at a cost which seems unbelievable today—£15,000. This structure was not only a fine additional attraction but it buttressed the secondary sea wall which had been built on top of James Brogden's original defence line. The Council then went on to develop the Eastern Promenade, connecting the sea front with New Road. To do this the workmen had to brick up and fill in the entrance to the inner dock, effectively also creating a lagoon which became known as the Salt Lake. At the northern extremity of the new thoroughfare the old allotments near the gasworks were converted into Griffin Park, named after Mr W. J. Griffin, several times Chairman of the Council. The Park became one of the main attractions of the town, replete with bowling greens, tennis courts and a children's playground. The new promenade also helped to alleviate the traffic on Station Hill, frequently brought to a halt by the level-crossing. In the summer the railway was extremely busy, not only with normal traffic but with excursion trains from places as far away as the Midlands, a state of affairs aggravated by the fact that the original station in South Road had been dismantled and a new one built where the present Port Way now stands. As a result the crossing gates seemed to be permanently in use, much to the enjoyment of local youngsters who, from vantage points on the footbridge, specialised in the art of dropping stones down the funnels of the slow-moving locomotives.

Just after the termination of the war the fairground was built on the site of the old ballast tip. Starting with two World War I R.A.F. hangers and the original Figure Eight ride (erected in 1920 but now sadly demolished) the area quickly developed into what we know today as the Coney Beach Amusement Park. On Coney Beach itself a long line of bathing huts appeared, for it was then considered immodest to undress in public. Mounted on wheels they were drawn by horses up and down the beach according to the state of the tide.

Not far from the fairground the newly-formed Salt Lake was developed. Originally the inner harbour this became a mecca for swimmers (many a Porthcawl child was taught to swim by Mr Cowie) and for those who liked to row and sail, small boats were available for hire at reasonable prices. Many successful regattas were held there in the holiday season, but impecunious youngsters had to gravitate to the Billy Pool on the rocks near the Seabank Hotel, where they taught themselves to swim.

During the inter-war years paddle steamers called regularly at Porthcawl. Docking at the breakwater, they took many holidaymakers and residents on trips to the resorts in Devon and Somerset. Sunday was the most popular day for at that time the Sunday Closing Act prohibited the drinking of alcoholic beverages on the Sabbath, and the bars of the steamers were open as soon as the ships got under way. Tickets for the outings could be purchased at the small round building near the slipway, which was once the dock office. For holiday-makers who wished to remain safely ashore relaxation could be obtained by sitting on a deck chair on the promenade or on The Green, where they could hear a brass band or an orchestra playing on the bandstand. Unhappily the bandstand, too, has disappeared, although its foundations can still be seen in the

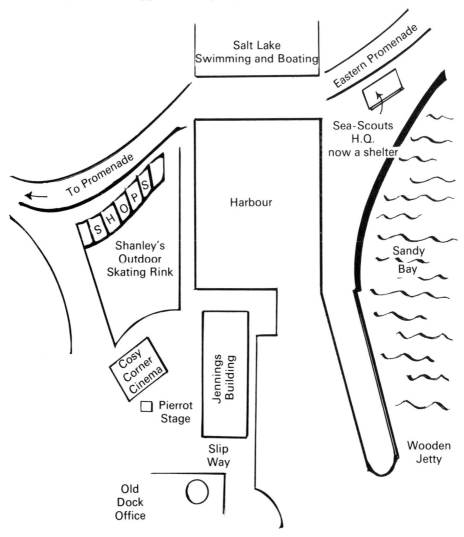

15 Diagram of old Cosy Corner site

centre of The Green. If they tired of music they could wander down the prom. and listen to Tommy, the ventriloquist's puppet, with performances twice a day, or watch the parades of bazooka bands. These bands, dressed in cheaply-made but colourful costumes, were a notable sight during the inter-war years when the Great Depression badly affected the valleys. To utilize their spare time the miners and their families formed the bands which marched to tunes played on the bazooka, a peculiarly American instrument which made a sound like air being blown through a paper-covered comb.

Another part of the dock developed at this time was the area near the outer basin, which became known as Cosy Corner. This name appears to be an anomaly for the site is one of the most exposed in the resort and anything but cosy in the winter, but it came about because a comfortable cinema (again made out of an aeroplane hangar) was erected there in 1923 by Mr George Beynon. The Cosy Corner Cinema showed all the latest films and many repertory companies put on excellent productions on its wide stage. The cinema also became the original venue for productions by the newly-formed Porthcawl Amateur Operatic and Dramatic Society, started by Mr Beynon, Mr Trevor Hughes and the writer's father, Oliver Morgan, who was its first musical director. Before being demolished the building had a short career as a roller-skating rink. Roller-skating was very popular in the 'thirties, for Jenning's building was also used as an indoor rink, and an even larger outdoor one was constructed by Michael Shanly, an amusement caterer, on the nearby dockside. Skates could be hired quite cheaply and beginners instructed by Mr and Mrs Jackson. Many events were held there, including roller-skating hockey matches. To cater for the needs of the hundreds of people who went there, several wooden shops were constructed on the western side of this rink, selling a myriad of goods ranging from buckets and spades to Porthcawl Rock and ice cream. Sadly all this was also demolished, but the site was later turned into a pleasant green replete with a children's paddling pool. It is also worth recalling that the Beynon family owned two other cinemas in the town: the Casino (now the Stoneleigh Club) and the Coliseum (later turned into a supermarket), although these conversions did not come about until the advent of television.

Not to be out-done by other resorts Porthcawl even had its own aerodrome between the wars. Situated on a field running parallel with Locks Lane it was started by a Newton garage owner and aviator, Mr George Pine, who possessed a Fox-Moth aeroplane, later increased to two. Flights around the bay cost 2s 6d (12 ½p), trips as far as Swansea 5s (25p), but looping the loop was a little extra. Occasionally flying circuses visited the field with a weird and wonderful collection of aircraft, and many a thrilling flying display was put on for the benefit of residents and holiday-makers. During the summer months the nearby Locks Common was enlivened by the arrival of many Territorial Army units, who set up camp there. Led by military bands they took part in route marches around the town. Infantrymen practised their rifle-shooting on the rifle range on Newton Burrows and the cavalry put on displays of tent-pegging and complicated manoeuvres on the common itself—good training to face the future mechanical might of Hitler's armies. Camping holidays were also popular amongst the civilian population in those days—in 1939 no less than 10,000 people set up tent in various fields around the town. For those who wanted a more luxurious holiday there were now many fine hotels: the Seabank, the Esplanade, the Porthcawl, the Atlantic, the Pier and Fairways. There were also many boarding houses in Mary Street and Esplanade Avenue, and to keep the wolf from the door in those depressed days quite a few housewives 'took in visitors'.

Meanwhile many South Wales miners, ravaged by illnesses caused by their dangerous and unhealthy occupation, were rejuvenated by a stay at The Rest Convalescent Home. There they were well looked after by the matron and her staff, and the pure Porthcawl air no doubt aided their recuperation. Also enjoying the life-giving air were the members of the nearby Royal Porthcawl Golf Club. Honoured by the title 'Royal', bestowed by Edward VII in 1909, the links course was becoming known world-wide for the excellence of its fairways and greens. Many important international events were staged there, attracting hundreds of spectators and thus adding to the wealth of the town.

By 1939 the resident population had grown to 7,000, a figure expanded three-fold by visitors in the summer months, brought to the resort by the many attractions and amenities enumerated in this chapter. Many older residents, looking back on that era, are still amazed that so much was done in such a short while and are saddened at the demise of many things that created a great deal of happiness both for themselves and for the thousands of holiday-makers who came to the resort then. No doubt Porthcawl would have gone on expanding and multiplying these amenities, for towards the end of the 'thirties trade generally was reviving. Unfortunately much of the extra cash in people's pockets was the result of the government's increased expenditure on re-armament, for the threat of another war hung like a cloud on the horizon. Porthcawlians, along with the rest of the country's population, listened on their wirelesses to the ranting and raving of an ex-corporal of the German army who had made himself the head of that powerful state, and the more perspicacious of them knew that war was not far away. And when it came it turned out to be a war which changed many things in Porthcawl, not all of them for the better. To end on another unhappy note one other sad event must be mentioned: the death of Miss Lucy Brogden, James Brogden's daughter. After the loss of the family fortune she took a small cottage (Rose Cottage) in Philadelphia Road, where she spent the rest of her days breeding bloodhounds to augment her small income. Always pleasant but shabbily dressed, she was a well-known sight in the town, where she could be seen every day exercising her small pack of animals on the ends of a myriad of hopelessly intertwined leads. When she died Porthcawl's links with the unfortunate Brogden family finally came to an end.

12.

World War II and after

When World War II broke out in September 1939 development in the town stopped almost immediately. Now there was conscription (a hard lesson learnt in the 1914-18 War when the flower of the country's youth had been decimated on the fields of Flanders) and within a few months of the war starting, hotels and empty private houses were commandeered by the military. A large aerodrome was built at Stormy Down to train bomber crews and a marine base set up near the outer harbour. Evacuees arrived from London and everyone had to carry a gas mask, even the horses, a surprising number of which were still to be seen.

For a time the 'phoney war' meant that little seemed to happen, but in 1940 the British Expeditionary Force was driven out of France at Dunkirk. The British army was joined by many French, Belgian and Dutch units, and soldiers of the Royal Dutch Army came to Porthcawl, where they became familiar figures in their blue-green uniforms. The Blitzkrieg then started, with Swansea being devastated by air-raids. The bombers tried to get at the Arsenal, built just before the war near Bridgend, but it had been skilfully sited in a misty area and so little damage was done. Many Porthcawl people, especially women, were employed at this huge munitions factory.

As the war spread further afield, American troops were billeted in the area, many of them in large tented camps near the perimeter of the parish. For the civilians life became drab, with food rationing, clothing coupons and little or no petrol for private cars, most of which had to be laid up for the duration of hostilities. All iron railings and unused structures made of metal were dismantled to provide raw material for armaments, and the black-out added to the gloom. Eventually British, Canadian and American troops re-entered Europe and as though overnight Porthcawl became denuded of soldiers. Two atomic bombs on Hiroshima and Nagasaki finished the war and Porthcawl, along with the rest of the victorious but tired country, tried to return to normal. This was not easy, however, for rationing and shortages went on for many years after the cessation of hostilities, but gradually conditions got better. A new list of those killed in the war was inscribed on the town's cenotaph and Armistice Day changed to the first Sunday in November. The second 'war to end war' was finally over.

Slowly things got back to normal but rarely to what they had been before. The Salt Lake had been filled in and become a car park, so there was no swimming and boating such as had enlivened the inter-war years. The buildings on the Cosy Corner site (except for Jenning's building) had been torn down and the pastime of roller-skating disappeared for ever. Gone, too, was the aerodrome at Locks Lane, and also the paddle steamers, many of which had done sterling service in the evacuation from Dunkirk. They returned later, but their trips were never as numerous or frequent as pre-war. Even the bandstand on The Green had been taken away, its railings having been used to make munitions, so there was no more music by brass bands and orchestras. The two remaining cinemas, the Casino and the Coliseum, succumbed before the onslaught of television, and a painful blow came when the Beeching plan denuded Porthcawl of its railway. The station was dismantled, the rails torn up and the tunnel at Nottage blocked at both ends. The sight of a dozen excursion trains waiting on the sidings to take hundreds of holiday-makers back home would never again be seen. The Portway took the place of the main line and the age of the motor car and luxury coach was well under way. The loss of the railway also meant that in periods of heavy snow the resort could sometimes be cut off, and indeed during one winter it had to be supplied by sea. The closure had one good effect, however. The level crossing and the signal box on station hill were done away with and the area became a shopping precinct. All these losses, plus the fact that there was a shortage of bricks, timber, cement and paint (badly bombed areas had priority for re-building) made it difficult to repair the ravages of neglect caused by nearly six years of war.

Nevertheless Porthcawlians still looked forward to the future with optimism, and hoteliers and boarding-house owners did what they could to refurbish their properties after the assault of hundreds of army boots. Fondly it was hoped that visitors would soon return in force, and that pre-war conditions would prevail once more. But a change in holiday habits was already taking place. During the inter-war years thousands of people had come to Porthcawl to enjoy a camping holiday: now the tents were being replaced by trailer caravans. At first their number was small, and they were placed haphazardly but inconspicuously among the sand-dunes near Coney Beach and Treco Bay. To cater for this type of holiday-maker the Council purchased 56 acres of land in 1946, but then came the privately-developed Treco Bay caravan site—250 acres which stretched from 100 yards east of Mackworth Road to the eastern boundary of the parish. This area rapidly filled with stationary caravans and became, in time, the biggest caravan complex in Europe. To accommodate as many caravans as possible, the sand-dunes were bull-dozed to form a flat, uniform surface, much to the sorrow of many Porthcawlians who remembered the area as a wild but beautiful part of the coastline. The new complex became virtually self-sufficient, with its own shops, bars, cafes, dance halls and entertainment centres. There was even a cinema, a church and a swimming pool. Caravan holidays became very popular, especially among the South Wales miners who could enjoy their stay without hotel or boarding house restrictions, but the effect on Porthcawl was marked. Few caravan dwellers came into the town to shop or make use of the facilities there, with the result that those who made their living providing accommodation saw their trade greatly reduced. Ladies who previously 'kept visitors' in private houses, as in pre-war days, found no customers at all.

The creation of the caravan parks therefore had a bad initial effect on the

16   Treco Bay before the caravan parks were built

town, but final calamity was averted by another post-war development. Porthcawl had for years been to some extent a dormitory town, with people commuting to the business and industrial centres of Cardiff, Swansea and Bridgend. Now a huge steelworks was brought into commission at Port Talbot—the Steel Company of Wales. The works, referred to as 'Treasure Island' by South Walians because of the wealth it generated meant that many of its employees came to Porthcawl to reside, attracted there by its advantages, principally fine beaches and clean, unpolluted air. This brought about an infusion of the life-giving blood demanded by every town—extra money for the rates. The result was that the town suddenly began to expand again, Porthcawl to the west as far as Rest Bay, Nottage along the West Road area, and Newton to both north and east. So rapid was this expansion there seemed a danger that the two ancient villages might have lost their identity, for it became difficult to spot the demarcation lines between them and the town itself, but happily they have managed to retain their character.

Other changes came about because of another factor: the reorganisation in 1974 of the Glamorgan County boundaries. This large county was split up into three smaller ones, designated West, Mid and South Glamorgan, with Mid Glamorgan being further divided into boroughs, of which Ogwr was one; and immediately the old Porthcawl Urban District Council was stripped of many of its powers. No longer could it plan the grandiose schemes which its predecessor had so successfully brought to fruition, such as the building of the Pavilion, the Lower Promenade and Griffin Park. Now decisions had to be taken by a much larger council composed of members who resided in other parts of the borough, and who naturally placed the requirements of their own area first. At this time, too, Porthcawl lost its parliamentary connection with Aberavon, being amalgamated instead with Bridgend.

Nevertheless Porthcawl has continued to develop along lines which give pleasure to the majority of its inhabitants. Much of the surrounding country-side, such as the areas in the vicinity of Sker, Newton Boroughs and Merthyr Mawr Warren, remain largely unspoiled. Locks Lane may have been partially invaded by houses, but most of the original ancient lanes are still in existence and surrounded by fields, as any walk along Zig-Zag, Ty'n-y-Caeau or Moor Lane will testify. Many of the old farm houses are still standing, imparting a rural atmosphere to much of the area, and there are always the fine beaches and open spaces such as Locks Common and The Green. The villages of Newton and Nottage also retain their old-world charm. There is still a wide, sweeping Promenade with the Pavilion as its centrepiece and a good shopping centre along the streets planned by James Brogden, John Street, Well Street and Lias Road, with further good facilities at Station Hill and New Road.

The habits of holiday-makers may have changed in that the majority of them obtain accommodation in the caravans, but the town itself is attracting more and more visitors. They may not stay a long time for foreign holidays have taken their toll on sea-side resorts all over the country, but many come for short periods, and for this they are served by excellent hotels and boarding houses. The growing popularity of Porthcawl can also be seen any Sunday or Bank Holiday when the car parks are full and all parking spaces along the promenades and West Drive occupied by vehicles. The Rest Convalescent Home is still functioning, but mercifully miners suffering from chest complaints are now rare, their place being taken by patients of a different kind, especially pensioners who seem to benefit greatly from their stay.

Porthcawl has also developed into a notable conference centre, the Pavilion being frequently in demand as a venue for political parties and the South Wales miners. The miners, especially, have a particular liking for Porthcawl, for the resort has had a long and happy relationship with the nearby mining communi-ties. Big events such as golfing tournaments at the Royal Porthcawl Golf Club and the Pyle and Kenfig Golf Club attract large numbers of visitors, as do bowling events at Griffin Park and fishing competitions when the coastline is thick with anglers. In the main, however, Porthcawl is now a residential town, attracting a growing number of people who come and live within its environs, especially those who have retired from work. The latter group find the place particularly beneficial for most of the town and the surrounding countryside is flat, making it easy for the elderly to get about. For those who are still active or at work commuting has been made easy by the advent of the M4, which passes very close to the parish boundary. The town is also fortunate in having a large number of societies which cater for almost any need, ranging from such occupations as music appreciation and painting to floral arrangement and dog-handling. (A full list of clubs and societies is given at the end of this book.)

Evening classes are held at the Comprehensive School, and sport is well catered for with clubs for the playing of rugby, association football, hockey and cricket. A fine County Lending Library was built in 1962 (at a cost of £12,000) to cater for a population which by 1987 had expanded to nearly 16,000. Religious denominations are well represented, as they have been since the early days of the parish, but these will be dealt with more fully later.

Another link with Porthcawl's past can still be seen in the harbour area. The original outer dock is still in existence but now it caters for small boats which use the facilities for sailing and fishing. Their exit and entrance is still guarded by that epitaph to James Brogden, the Porthcawl breakwater, a structure which has withstood the fiercest of storms for over a hundred years and will probably continue to do so for the next hundred, if not for ever. Nearby is another of James Brogden's undertakings, the inner dock, which he tried for so many years to make successful. After World War II it became nothing more than a rubble-filled eight-acre site, and many schemes have been put forward to revitalise and beautify it. At the time of writing other plans are being formulated and it is to be hoped that the company awarded the contract will be mindful of the history of the area so that James Brogden, if he could see the final result, would be well pleased.

13.

Religion

A.   *The Churches*

If an early Celtic cell had existed in Nottage its importance would have been over-shadowed when Newton Church was built. The Normans were as unyielding in religion as they were in battle, and the only beliefs they permitted were those based on the doctrines of Rome: all else was heresy. Thus Newton Church became the centre of the Catholic faith in the parish and remained so for several centuries until the Reformation changed the administration, if not the ritual, of the church in England and Wales. Obeying Henry VIII Newton-Nottage, along with every community in the land, adopted the Anglican faith.

Since its original construction either towards the end of the twelfth century or the beginning of the thirteenth, the church of St John has been altered, strengthened and refurbished in order to cater for the gradually increasing congregation; but it has retained its basic early Norman characteristics. The bells were replaced by new ones, eventually becoming a peal of six, the

17   The first All Saints Church, constructed of corrugated iron

graveyard doubled in size and in 1843 a person was appointed to look after the clock at a salary of one guinea a year, subsequently cut to sixteen shillings (80p), reason not given. Even when other denominations became numerous in the parish the church remained very much part of the village and for many years was the only place of Anglican worship. No doubt this would have remained the case, but when the new dock was constructed and the early town of Porthcawl developed around it there came a demand for a second church near the centre of this new hive of activity. A Sailors' Mission Church was accordingly erected near the dock, catering for the dockers and tramroad men as well as for the seafaring community, and the Rev. Augustus Rickards Blundell was appointed Chaplain in 1866. Within two years, however, the tiny building became too small for the rapidly increasing population, and so when the National School was opened in 1873 (itself an Anglican institution) worshippers went there, holding both Sunday and week-day services. But this place also, became too small and when Lord Wimborne offered land in Victoria Avenue for the construction of a proper church the chance was seized with alacrity. The first building was made of iron and lasted from 1892 to 1914, by which time the population of the town was such that there was no alternative but to build an edifice which would cater for existing and future congregations. The iron church was dismantled and given to the Anglicans in the Maesteg area, who wanted it for a mission hall, and on the site was constructed the present stone building. The new All Saints Church was built in fifteenth century Gothic style, the stone being obtained from the Forest of Dean and the roof slates from Dinorwic. It had seating for a congregation of six hundred and cost just under £10,000. The consecration was conducted by the Bishop of Llandaff in February 1914 and additional parts such as the lady chapel, choir vestry and south porch were added later.

Thus by the outbreak of World War I both Newton and Porthcawl had an Anglican church, but Nottage was still without one, possibly because it had long been a bastion of nonconformity. This state of affairs was rectified at the instigation of the Rector, Canon William Roach who, just after the second world war, erected a temporary church army hut on land given by the late Mr J. K. Blundell. In 1948 a proper small church was built there, dedicated to St David, and has been active ever since.

One interesting and unusual fact is that although there were eventually three Anglican churches in the parish there has never been a proper manse. This is undoubtedly because most of the early rectors were not resident in Newton-Nottage. Indeed, between 1743 and 1833 they were nearly all lords of one or other of the manors. A rectory was built on land given by Lord Wimborne in 1908, but this became a school, and even today incumbents live in ordinary houses.

Beginning in Elizabethan times, when the enemy was Spain, Catholics in Britain were not tolerated. To worship they had to meet in secret and the priests forced to adopt disguises. Two of these priests were harboured by the Turbervilles at Sker House, where they had special recesses called priest-holes, and one, Father Evans, was caught and executed at Cardiff in 1679. It was not until the nineteenth century that Catholics were really allowed to worship openly without fear of reprisal and it was not until 1904 that a meeting place came into being in Porthcawl. It was established by Miss Clara Waddle, who erected a wooden building in New Road. This became known as the Waddle Hall, the small early Catholic community being served by Canon Crowe, O.S.B. Enlarged in 1908 the hall also became the headquarters of various societies such as the Girl Guides; and later a new, modern church was built, appropriately named *Our Lady, Star of the Sea.*

B.   *Early Chapels*

To understand the formation of nonconformist denominations in the area it is necessary to go back to the seventeenth century. Nottage had long been a preaching centre for dissidents who opposed the doctrines of the established church, and one man, Lewis Thomas, became the leader of the *Calvinistic Baptists* in Swansea. Later he came to live at Mŵr, in Moor Lane, and held services there, his devoted band of followers becoming known as 'the brothers of Mŵr.' When Charles II was restored to the throne severe penalties were inflicted on the dissenters, many of whom fled to America to obtain freedom of worship. Others refused to conform and went on meeting clandestinely. Richard Cradock's house, for example, became a secret meeting place where as many as thirty people gathered. Later Parliament forbade the assembly of more than five people for religious worship, but the meetings went on. In 1672 the Declaration of Indulgence suspended the worst penalties against dissenters and allowed persons to preach under licence. Two such licences were granted in the parish, one to Watkin Cradock, an Independent, and another to Howel Thomas, a Baptist. Later still the Toleration Act permitted religious assemblies except for Roman Catholics and Unitarians. Nottage responded by having meetings in private houses and other men became ministers, including James Lewis and Thomas Leyson. The famous Hywel Harris also formed a society in the village which, by the end of the end of the eighteenth century had become a centre of Nonconformity, with no less than four sects represented: Baptists, Independents, Presbyterians and Methodists, a remarkable feat considering how small the population was. The first to have a proper chapel were the Baptists who, in 1788, converted a house for that purpose, the first minister being David Powell, who came from Felinfoel. By the end of the century, however, the congregation had split up because of doctrinal differences, the Particular Baptists seceding and the General Baptists remaining in possession of the chapel.

The first Unitarian minister in Nottage, then closely linked with a sister chapel in Wick, was the Rev. Evan Lloyd. Appointed in 1806 he was to remain minister for forty years; indeed except for a small gap of five years the Lloyd family were to serve the Nottage cause for a remarkable period of 120 years.

Meanwhile in Newton the *Independent* preachers were not having much success, but by 1808 they were holding services at a house called Bethel, the first minister being William Williams. Later the members took steps to construct a proper chapel. This was Hope, opened in 1828, subsequently enlarged and renovated. By 1890 it had a congregation of 78, but by now many of the members were living in the growing town of Porthcawl, so there was a demand for a Welsh chapel there. When it was formed Hope became an English cause to cater for a population which, even in the early days, was largely English speaking.

C.   *Later Chapels*

The *Calvinistic Methodists* started in 1859 with a Sunday School in a loft of the Victoria public house. Then they were offered land in South Road by Mrs George Sibbering and building started five years later. The congregation was too small to support a minister so other denominations helped out by providing preachers for forty weeks in the year. Eventually Bethel had its first minister, the Rev. Watkin Joseph, who was also a chaired bard. Services were in Welsh, but with the influx of new workers the town was becoming more English every day. The Rev. Joseph asked permission to preach in English, but his request was refused, so he left to become minister of the English Congregational chapel which had been opened on New Road in 1872. Many of the congregation went with him and Bethel was left weak in numbers (6 in 1881). Gradually, however, the congregation increased in size and by 1951 had reached 115.

The *Baptist* cause in Porthcawl was at first weak, with members meeting in cottages and a room in the Railway Tavern in South Road. They were greatly helped in their early days by the minister and congregation of Pisgah Baptist Church in Pyle, and by 1867 they were considering building a chapel which was to be called Gilgal. The chapel was opened in 1869 as a branch of Pisgah, but three years later it became a separate church. After many vicissitudes the movement became a strong one, the congregation outgrowing the original building, and so in 1923 the new Gilgal, a fine large church capable of seating 750 was opened in Park Avenue, its pastor on that important occasion being the Rev. T. Arthur Davies.

At first the *Wesleyans* had a small mission church near the docks started, it was said, after an open-air service of thanksgiving for sailors rescued from a ship in a storm. Meetings were subsequently held in an upper room of a storehouse. Later they were given land at the junction of Lias Road and John Street by James Brogden on which they built their chapel. Enlarged and improved over the years, the Wesleyan church amalgamated with Highfield United Reformed Church in 1984, after which it became known as Trinity, the first minister of the combined congregations being the Rev. Colin E. Richards. Ideally sited in the middle of the town Trinity has become one of the most active denominations in the parish.

The growing number of English-speaking people in Porthcawl in the nineteenth century brought about a demand for an *English Independent* cause and for this reason Mrs Mary Caroline Brogden gave a site on New Road (near the present Masonic Temple). The chapel was completed in 1871 and the first minister was the Rev. Watkin Joseph, who had come from Bethel bringing with him many of the latter chapel's congregation. In 1916 the land on which the chapel stood was conveyed to the Masonic Hall Co. Ltd., and so for a time services were held at Stoneleigh and the Coliseum cinema. Later a disused roller-skating rink was renovated and converted into a proper chapel, and in 1918 Highfield Congregational church opened its doors, the first minister being the Rev. J. P. Southwell. As previously stated, after being a separate cause in the town for 113 years, the English United Reformed Church joined forces with the Wesleyans to form one church, Trinity.

The *Welsh Congregational* cause already had a firm base in Hope chapel, Newton. To try and start their movement in the growing town of Porthcawl meetings were first held (between 1916 and 1919) in a room in the Y.M.C.A. but later members moved to the Celtic Cafe in John Street. Then they obtained a plot of land at Fenton Place on which was a store house. This was refurbished and used until 1931 by which time the congregation numbered 125, the Rev. David Morris continuing in charge. In that same year the present Tabernacl was built, also at Fenton Place, a fine structure costing just over £4,300 and capable of seating 600.

The *English Presbyterian* movement was originally formed by members amicably seceding from Bethel. Services in English continued to be held for a while at Bethel, then the small congregation moved to a room also in the Celtic Cafe in John Street. Increasing numbers strengthened the sect and so a site for a chapel was obtained in Arlington Road. It was completed in 1925, the first minister being the Rev. W. J. Davies.

The *Plymouth* or *Christian Brethren* cause started in Porthcawl largely at the instigation of Mr Alex Smith, a coastguard who came to Porthcawl about 1903. At first meetings were held on the sea front but later members hired a room in a house in John Street. The expanding numbers brought about a desire to build a proper chapel, and a piece of land was obtained in Lias Road. Completed in 1909 this was the present Gospel Hall, which was subsequently considerably enlarged.

Much later than any of the chapels mentioned above, Noddfa in Philadelphia Road was not started until 1939 and, in spite of the oubreak of war, was allowed to be completed. Fortunately for members the cost then was only £5,000, an amount paid off within fourteen years. It was opened in 1940, the first resident minister being the Rev. S. L. Davies, B.A., B.D. The *Welsh Baptist* cause was therefore firmly re-established in the town largely as a result of the efforts and determination of the late Rev. T. Thomas, B.A.

14.

Education

For centuries succeeding governments were afraid that education for the masses would lead to revolution or at the very least to too much power in the wrong hands, so it was left to well-meaning men to provide the first schools for the children of the poor. Unfortunately the poor did not always respond, for the pressure to get children working was great, so the public schools ultimately became repositories for the sons of the wealthy.

In the meantime, in Wales, Gruffydd Jones was starting his Circulating Charity Schools, brought into being mainly to teach religious knowledge through the medium of Welsh to both children and adults. These schools were, as the name implies, peripatetic establishments, travelling to various parts of the country usually in the winter months when there was less work on the farms. There were two such schools in our area, one in Nottage and one in Newton. Active between 1738 and 1763, the number of pupils varied between 30 and 84, but these schools only touched the fringe of the problem, although they did teach people to read.

The influence of Thomas Charles was also seen in Nottage, for a Sunday School was established there in 1818, later increased to four. But these schools were operative only once a week and the instruction was again mainly religious. The only chance the children of poorer parents had of obtaining knowledge of 'the three R's' (reading, writing and arithmetic) was to be sent to what became known as 'Dame Schools.' These were one-teacher establishments, usually held in a room of a cottage, the teacher invariably being an elderly man or woman with just a smattering of education. The fees were about one penny (½p) per subject per week. There were three such schools in Porthcawl, one of them becoming quite well known. This was run by a Thomas Thomas (known to the children and parents alike as Tom Tom), and held above a blacksmith's shop on the dock-side. After 1850 he moved to 5, Lias Cottages, which became known as Old School House, and was still in being as late as 1859. The youngest daughters of the Rev. E. D. Knight also tried to help the children of the parish by holding classes at Nottage Court in the evenings.

No doubt spurred on by the Methodist Circulating Schools, albeit with the main intention of keeping their congregations strong, the non-conformist bodies began their own British Schools and, not to be out-done, the Church of England responded with National Schools. One of the latter came into existence in Newton as early as 1811, known as Mrs Elias' School, and another in 1835 (Mrs Jones' School). The assistants for these two good ladies were Miss Rawlinson and Miss Eagles. These were proper schools in that they were operative every week-day, but the pupils' parents still had to pay for instruction. There was also a private school in Porthcawl and four Sunday Schools, one Anglican and one Methodist in the town, one Baptist in Nottage and one Independent in Newton.

This was the position when the Report of the Commissioners of Inquiry into the State of Education in Wales was published in 1847. Known as The Blue Books because of the colour of the covers, and referred to by Welsh people as 'Brâd y Llyfrau Gleision' ('Treachery of the Blue Books') because the report was so scathing, the publications nevertheless give a vivid picture of the educational facilities in the parish in the middle of the nineteenth century. They show that only three-quarters of the school accommodation was occupied and that only a third of the children attended school. Of this third the majority of pupils left before completing one year. Of the Sunday Schools the Church of England class had fifteen pupils whereas the nonconformist establishments could boast of a total of 242. The day-schools referred to above were harshly dealt with in other respects. Mrs Elias, for example, was 65 and had been a housemaid. She was described as being 'somewhat intelligent, but spoke English incorrectly'. Her salary was £2-10s-0d (£2.50) per annum. Mrs Jones, who was paid £1-10s-0d (£1.50) per annum, was a 62 year old widow. The master of the private school fared little better, for although he 'appeared intelligent and wrote a fair hand' he, too, 'spoke English incorrectly.' His pupils were orderly, however, but had to endure a room that was 'miserably small and close.' The subjects in all three schools were reading, religious instruction and handwriting,

18 The National School, Lias Road

and only a few pupils did arithmetic. All had English books but Welsh was also used for instruction.

Hated though the Commissioners' Report was it had the effect of galvanizing people into action. The National Society gave a grant of £96 for the erection of a proper school, and this came into being on a site near Newton Green (where a beer house called the Harriet used to be). Completed in 1848 with accommodation for 96 children, the first teachers were probably Henry and Elizabeth Monro. Later Miss Selina Harris took over and a report on the school in 1874 spoke of education up to the grade of Standard III. The school remained in being until 1907, when the attendance was 70 pupils.

In 1870 the Elementary Education Act provided for the setting up of locally elected school boards. The then Rector (the Rev. E. D. Knight) called a meeting with the intention of building a new school in Porthcawl, with the result that in 1873 the National School in Lias Road was built, 'a handsome and commodious' structure. The first headmaster was Mr William Rees and a subsequent report described the school as 'extremely well conducted' with instruction being 'regular, systematic and efficient.' It was soon placed in the category of 'Excellent Mixed Schools', and when fees were abolished towards the end of the century the number of pupils grew to 250.

Another Education Act in 1902 abolished School Boards and made church schools rate-maintained. They were placed under the County Councils and so the National School became known (in 1924) as the Porthcawl Nottage Council School. In the meantime the original Newton National school had been carrying on its work, but in 1908 the Glamorgan Council completed a new council school in New Road, and so the Newton children were transferred to it. It started with 144 pupils and its first headmaster was Mr Job Baker.

By this time the population of the town was growing considerably, which meant that the Lias Road School was becoming too small for the number of children, and so a new building was planned in Suffolk Place. The foundations were laid but the outbreak of war in 1939 stopped all progress, and it was not until after World War II that the school was completed, the headmaster being Mr A. D. Perkins. In the meantime, now bulging at the seams, the National School carried on, educating large numbers of children and also being used as a focal point by townspeople who held various meetings there. This fine old building, constructed in the shape of a cross, was eventually demolished and a superstore built on the site. The only reminder that a school was once there is the name of an adjoining street—Old School Road.

In 1933 a new kind of school—a Senior School—was started in Park Avenue. Built originally for 400 pupils between the ages of 11 and 14 its first headmaster was the late Mr Leonard Higgins, O.B.E., M.A. the author of 'Newton Nottage and Porthcawl'. It then became a Secondary Modern School and the leaving age was raised to 15, later to 16. When the Scholarship Examination (the 'Eleven-plus') was abolished in the 1970s it was progressively turned into a Comprehensive School with a pupil population that at one time approached 1600. Mr D. G. Ebsworth, B.Sc., M.A. was its first principal. Also to cater for the increasing number of children two other junior schools were established, one in Nottage called West Park Primary School, first headmaster Mr D. H. David, B.A., and one to serve the growing council estate. The latter was called Porthcawl Primary School and its first headmaster was Mr Islwyn Griffiths, B.A.

Mention has already been made of early 'Dame Schools' but as the town became larger and more prosperous private schools of a much superior nature sprang up. Probably the most prestigious was the Porthcawl College, a boarding school for boys set up in Sea Bank House (previously the home of James and Mary Brogden). The headmaster was the Rev. J. J. Newell, M.A. Not so large but of equal standing was the Esplanade School for Girls (principals the Misses Jones) situated on the sea front. Later, under the Brills, it moved to Stoneleigh and was a well-known girls' boarding school for many years. (Interestingly, when Stoneleigh was built its front wall incorporated an iron drinking fountain which was later moved to the shelter opposite the Seabank Hotel where it can be seen today—now without water). There was also a preparatory school for boys run by the Misses Garsed in Gordon Road, Later they moved to Moorlands, a boarding and day school for girls which lasted until World War II. Miss Howell had a High School for Girls in the Rhyll and Miss Harrison a boys' school in South Road. Between the wars others appeared: Mrs Corfield's St Catherine's College, Miss John's preparatory in Mary Street and in 1929

Miss Howell built the Porthcawl College for Girls in Lougher Gardens—then within sight of the sea.

All the schools mentioned in the last paragraph have now ceased to function, but two other private schools are still in existence and 'recognised' by the Ministry of Education. St John's School, Newton, was opened in 1923 as a day and boarding preparatory school for boys, its first headmaster being Mr Gwilym Lewis, M.A. St Clare's Convent School for Girls was opened in Clevis House in 1938 with five pupils. The principal was then Sister Teresa Mary. Expansion was prevented by the outbreak of World War II but during hostilities many evacuees came from London to reside at the school and by 1951 the number of pupils had grown to 51 and St Clare's became a proper boarding establishment. Both these private schools can boast a formidable record in scholastic successes.

15.

Administration

A.   The Councils

Local government in the parish began gradually as the lords of the manors and their courts relinquished over-sight over day-to-day matters, and by the beginning of the nineteenth century the parish council was well established. Its early officers were the churchwarden, the overseer of the poor, the surveyor of highways and, later, the constable. The first recorded meeting in Newton-Nottage took place in 1818 and was held in the church porch. Seventeen persons attended one of whom signed his name with a cross. It continued to meet erratically but by 1836 there were regular gatherings in private houses and various inns such as the Crown, the Farmers' Arms and the Lamb. Later meetings settled down in the church vestry and so the council also became known as the vestry. Its main duties were the levying of the poor rate, estimating a church rate to repair the church and (until 1835) organising gangs of villagers to maintain the roads. One of the first church wardens was Watkin Bevan, a member of a family whose ancestors went back for generations. Sundry other matters came up such as the appointment of a man to prevent animals straying on Newton Down (enclosed by then), selecting a school board to set up the National School and the levying of a special rate to provide a constable and pay part of the cost of the Quarter Sessions.

Until 1836 the parish remained responsible for the Elizabethan Poor Laws, the Overseer arranging relief to the sick and needy. This took the form of providing a poor house (on the site of Rock House in South Road), the payment of money or the authorising of the purchase of essential commodities. Thus in 1837 Hannah Thomas, aged 98, was given 4s. (20p) a week and a pair of blankets; Barbara Colman aged 85 4s. 6d. (22½p) a week and a pair of calico sheets; and Elinor David had an order for wine confirmed (reason not given). Pauper burials were authorised at a maximum cost of 21s (£1.05p) which had to include 15s (75p) for a coffin. The Overseer also had to ensure that paupers coming to the parish were promptly dispatched back to their original abodes and that the able-bodied did work of some kind. From 1837 onwards they could be sent to the Workhouse in Quarella Road, Bridgend. 'Lunatic parishioners' received 4s. (20p) a week.

As the century progressed the increasing population added to the burdens of the parish councils, and so in 1834 they were combined into 'Unions' administered by Boards of Guardians, with each parish contributing to a central fund. The Board met for the first time in the Town Hall, Bridgend in 1836. A Relieving Officer (David Davies) and a Medical Officer of Health (Dr Price Jacob) were appointed. The Newton-Nottage representative was Watkin Bevan. From then on the task of looking after the poor and the overall administration of such things as the water supply and sewage came more and more under the aegis of medical men and so will be dealt with more fully in the next section.

In 1893 the parish of Newton-Nottage was converted into a Local Government District with its own Local Board, which met for the first time in the National School. The chairman was the Rector, the Rev. William Jones, and Mr Edward David (of Scale and David, Solicitors, Bridgend) was appointed Clerk. Also appointed were the Medical Officer of Health (Dr. R. T. Williams) and the Inspector of Nuisances (Watkin Bevan.) This Board was the first elected government body in the parish and immediately it ran into the twin problems of the water supply and sanitation. The water supply question proved almost insoluble, although James Brogden had already had a go at it by piping water from his well near the gasworks to a retainer tank in Well Street, from which it went by pipes to the Brogden houses. He tried to sell the water to the Board, who turned the offer down because of cost. Acrimony ensued and was not alleviated even when the Local Government Act of 1894 abolished the Boards and brought in Urban District Councils with increased powers. The new P.U.D.C. (first Chairman John Grace) had its inaugural meeting in December 1894 and immediately plunged into the water battle. They tried to get a supply from Kenfig Pool but the Burgesses turned them down, so they piped water from Ffynnon Fawr. For eight years this well provided many Porthcawl houses with water, but the majority of dwellings still had to rely on their own wells, and it was not until 1906 that the Craig-yr-Aber supply was tapped. With a service reservoir at Tŷ-Coch this solved the problem for many years until in 1953 the Mid-Glamorgan Water Board took over the responsibility with a never-failing supply from Llyn Brianne.

19   The Pavilion under construction, 1931

A special Porthcawl Urban District Council Act was passed in 1914 empowering the local body to take decisions previously denied to it. Although the outbreak of war delayed these measures, steps were taken to purchase the gas undertakings (subsequently nationalised in 1949) and to maintain and improve the harbour and breakwater. Advantage was also taken to provide the many amenities enumerated in Chapter 11 such as the lower and eastern promenades, the Salt Lake, the Pavilion and Griffin Park, with the result that Porthcawl became a proper seaside resort. The Council also took over the management of Locks Common, ensuring that this fine open space would always remain free of any encroachment by buildings. A new cemetery was built in 1934 and in 1946 a start was made with a large council estate, tastefully planned around the lakes which had once been part of the Wilderness wetlands.

In 1920 the growth of the population meant an increase in the number of commitments and so two Wards were set up—East and West. The council had no proper premises at first, meetings being successively held in Dare's shop in John Street, Ocean House in Dock Street, Beeche Terrace on Station Hill, the Coliseum upper room (1912) and South Road (1936). The latter became the main Council Chambers for many years before moving to Victoria Avenue. Much to the regret of many Porthcawlians the 1974 reorganisation of Glamorgan County boundaries meant the relinquishing of many of the Council's powers, and now main decisions affecting the town are taken by Ogwr Borough Council.

B.   *Medical Health*

As previously mentioned Medical Officers of Health were first appointed in 1836, the governing body being the Bridgend and Cowbridge Board of Guardians, then responsible for Newton-Nottage. The cholera epidemic of 1848-9 resulted in the first Public Health Act which established Local Boards of Health, the one for this area being set up in Bridgend. Later the Board of Guardians was made the sanitary authority. Immediately its officers got down to the task of looking into the medical health of the various parishes and what they found must have appalled them even by the standards of the day. Newton-Nottage, for example, had a myriad of porous cesspits which frequently drained into the wells. Slops and rubbish were just thrown out of houses or on the nearest piece of vacant land. As a result there were frequent epidemics. An attempt was made to improve things, mainly by way of closing the worst wells and brick-lining others. Many cesspits were also repaired and made leak-proof, and in 1853 Dr. Richard Leahy, the then Medical Officer of Health, started a programme of vaccinations (eight at 1s 6d each). Later, in 1884, a Parochial Council was formed to ensure that the improvements were being carried out, one of the original members being James Brogden. He went ahead on his own and built an outfall to the town's beach. Called the 'sea serpent' it was completed in 1887 but unfortunately it did not work properly because many of the feeder drains were defective. The town went on smelling badly, particularly in the summer.

When the Local Government Board began its deliberations in 1893 its first act was to order the Medical Officer to suggest ways of improving things. This took the form of providing a sewage cart to regularly empty the cesspits, employing men to clean the drains and extending the 'sea serpent' to beyond low water mark. These measures resulted in some improvement but it was not until the Porthcawl Urban District Council was formed in 1894 that real progress was made. A loan was obtained to create a proper sewage system, which at first consisted of a main drain going to an irrigation ground on Newton Burrows, all feeder pipes to be regularly flushed by the Council water cart. In 1902 an outlet pipe was routed to discharge into the sea at Newton Point and all town drains diverted to this main system. Brogden's 'sea serpent' became an outlet for surface drains and storm water only. This system served the parish well for a number of years, but by the 1970's the continually expanding population meant that sewage was not being properly disposed of, particularly in the summer months when thousands of holiday makers descend on the town. The beaches, especially, have been badly affected. At the time of writing a new scheme has been suggested: to send all effluent to the treatment centre at Ogmore. This will entail pipes being laid underground across Newton Burrows and Merthyr Mawr Warren, something which can be accomplished without scarring the landscape if care is taken. When completed it should mean that Porthcawl's fine beaches will be pollution free. Thus the battle against disease waged by a long line of Medical Officers of Health, ably supported first by conscientious Inspectors of Nuisances and then by councillors and council officials, will at long last have been won.

16.

Wrecks

Few visitors to Porthcawl realise that the resort is situated on one of the most dangerous parts of the coastline of Britain, a fact emphasised with monotonous regularity every summer when the R.N.L.I. out-board rescue craft has to go to the aid of swimmers in difficulty, children on li-lo beds and anglers who have no idea of the strength of off-shore currents. Over the centuries countless lives have been lost in the dozen or so square miles between Sker Point in the west and the Tuskar Rocks in the east, and some of the most spectacular and poignant wrecks have occurred in the neighbourhood. A few of these have already been described in 'Porthcawl: its History and Development' but as that booklet will shortly be out of print and the accounts are so interesting they have been repeated in this chapter. Fortunately modern navigation aids and better weather forecasting have made such disasters a thing of the past, but it would be well to remember that the Bristol Channel still possesses a ferocity not dreamed of by those who have not witnessed it at first hand.

One of the earliest recorded wrecks—and one that caused a furore in the district—was that of *La Vainqueur* which was stranded on Sker Beach in 1753. It was a French vessel, bound from Lisbon to Le Havre carrying a cargo of 789 chests of oranges, 650 frails of figs, an unknown quantity of lemons and 84 expensive planks of Brazil wood. The captain had made the not unusual mistake of confusing the Bristol Channel with the English Channel. The furore was caused by the fact that the ship had come ashore near Sker House, land which at that time was being farmed by Isaac Williams, the father of Elizabeth, the real Maid of Sker (not to be confused with R. D. Blackmore's fictitious heroine). Isaac was also Constable of the Hundred of Newcastle and as such it was his duty to guard the cargo until the constable arrived, instead of which the merchandise disappeared alarmingly quickly—into Isaac's barns and under the sand of what is now the golf links so the local populace said. This was sour grapes, for if the locals had got to the stuff first it would have disappeared just as quickly. As it was they had to content themselves with tearing the wreck to pieces and taking away all the planking, riggings and iron work, even down to the last nail. This was poor recompense for not getting their hands on the real merchandise and Isaac became a hated man, so much so that for years afterwards he went in danger of his life. He was summoned to appear before a court of enquiry held at the Kenfig Town Hall, now the Prince of Wales Inn, but through clever legal work he was exonerated of all charges of wreck robbing— a decision which did not endear him to the populace, especially as a few days after the tragedy many oranges, lemons and figs were being sold in local markets. The authorities had no alternative but to draw up proclamations stating that wreck pilfering was a capital offence. The notices were read out in all nearby churches on Christmas Day and seventeen men were later charged. Eight of the crew had been rescued but the captain and two hands were drowned. Even the master's body was not inviolate. It was robbed of a silver watch, shoe buckles and 17 gold Portuguese pieces. The watch turned up a few days later at the shop of a local watchmaker, where it had been taken for repair.

One of the saddest stories is that of a troopship driven on the Scarweathers during a storm in 1798. The vessel had sailed from Bristol carrying several regiments of soldiers destined for service in Ireland, where they were to put down a rebellion and then defend the country against possible attack by French forces. The ship quickly broke up and, as there was no rescue service in being at the time, hundreds of men were drowned, their bodies ultimately being washed ashore all along the coast between Sker and Porth Cawl Point. A mass grave, just wide enough to take a man's body and two hundred yards long, was dug on farming land abutting what is now West Drive, and there the soldiers were laid to rest in their salt-sodden uniforms. Sad to relate no memorial stone was ever erected there and after some years the tragedy was forgotten and the land re-ploughed. Later still houses were built on the site and during their construction a workman found one of the skeletons. He cleaned it up and presented it to a local doctor who, not knowing the real facts, used it in his surgery for demonstration purposes.

Although not entailing a large loss of life the foundering of the *Malleny* was an equally poignant episode. An iron sailing ship bound for South Africa it had left Cardiff in 1866 laden with coal. She went out of control off Swansea in a gale and drifted back along the Glamorgan coast. The only means of communication between Swansea and the rest of South Wales in those days was by telegraph but the high winds had blown down the wires, and so no preparation for a rescue attempt was put in hand. The ship was driven ashore off Nash Point and all the crew, who were coloured, were drowned. The little daughter of the white captain was found in the arms of one of the coloured men. A heartless local inhabitant collected four corpses, took them to St Brides in his cart and, as black men were then a rarity in the country, displayed them to curious sightseers for threepence a look.

Just as distressing is the story of the *Narcissus*, a Lowestoft trawler, which ran into trouble off Porthcawl in 1916. The crew burnt everything they could lay their hands on, including the ropes, in an attempt to attract attention, but to no avail. The ship then drifted into Porthcawl harbour and came within a few feet of being saved. But the exhausted crew had no ropes to make fast and, amazing to relate, watching bystanders along the harbour walls had no ropes either. A gust of wind took the ship out towards the Black Rocks and, although a human chain saved one boy from the small boat which had been launched but overturned, the rest of the crew of four perished in the waves.

Some of the wrecks had a lighter side, as when the *Perseverance* ran aground at Sker in 1808. A brig running from Cork to Bristol she had a cargo of Irish whiskey. She quickly broke up but all sixty of the crew and passengers were saved. It was not long, however, before the beaches were littered with casks of the fiery liquid and it needs no imagination to guess what the reaction of the local population was. They were quickly on the scene and there was much running to and fro, some of the casks being buried in the sand for recovery later. Two of the looters decided that the best way to transport their illicit gains was to put it inside them and literally drank themselves to death. Eventually the cavalry arrived from Swansea to protect the cargo, and this so incensed the mob, who regarded themselves as cheated, vicious fights broke out all along the beach. So ugly were the scenes the Riot Act had to be read (yet again) in all the local churches. It is interesting to speculate what would happen if a similar incident occurred today.

Also interesting is the story of the figure-head of the *William Miles*. This figure-head was for many years placed in the garden of Myrtle Cottage in Poplar Avenue and many people will remember it. The *William Miles* came into collision in the Bristol Channel with a much larger ship, the *Brilliant*, which sliced off the figure-head, depositing it on its own deck. The figure-head was repaired, returned to its rightful owner, and once more graced the prow of the *William Miles*. This seemed an unlucky omen and, sure enough, the *William Miles* was wrecked off Porthcawl in 1833. The figure-head was again rescued and taken to a ship-building yard in the docks, later to be transferred to Myrtle Cottage. There it stayed for many years, a source of wonder to all the small children of the town. Then, mysteriously, it disappeared and has never been seen or heard of since.

Faced with the fact that for centuries people living on or near the coast regarded wrecks as fair game for plunder, the authorities resorted to various means to protect the cargoes. This took the form of sending troops or constables, but usually the procedure was so slow and cumbersome it was a certainty that most of the merchandise would have disappeared by the time the protecting force got to the scene of the disaster. A new scheme was required which would ensure prompt action, and with this in mind a 'Protecting Fellowship' was formed in the Swansea and Neath districts. This was a body of armed men, many of them mounted, standing by to go at short notice to any part of the coast if a wreck was threatened. It was called out in 1781 when the Venetian vessel, the *Caterina*, ran aground also at Sker. The ship's cargo of cotton was already disappearing fast into local hands when they arrived (includ-

20 The *Speedwell* with its crew

ing those of the farmer's wife at New Park Farm who was seen to hide several bales) so the Protecting Fellowship quickly put a guard on the ship. This resulted in a pitched battle and three people were killed. Many of the plunderers were rounded up and placed in prison, but, because of the risk of further attack to release them, were transferred to Hereford. There, at the Assizes, they were tried and one of them, John Webb, was hanged.

In spite of the fact that wrecks have occurred for centuries all round the coasts of Britain succeeding governments have never seen the necessity for providing rescue services. This was left to well-meaning people such as William Weston Young who kept a boat ready at all times at Newton to go to the aid of a stricken vessel, and it was not until 1830 that Porthcawl had its first proper lifeboat provided, as has always been the case, by money donated by wealthy benefactors or public donations. This was the *Dolphin*, which did yeoman service for thirty years, to be followed by the *Good Deliverance*, renamed the *Brave Robert Shedden* in 1871. Then came the *Chafyn Grove*, a gift from Miss

Grove and finally the *Speedwell*, which lasted from 1887 to 1902. The lifeboat station was on the seafront near the present Pier Hotel and the boats were taken to the slipway on carriages with large wheels. Propulsion was by oars and one has only to stand on the breakwater during a storm to realise the courage of those men who had no weapon to aid themselves other than their own strength.

Other means of rescue were made by a contraption called Breeches Buoy, a method fraught with difficulty because a line had first to be got to the ship. During a gale the rocket carrying the line could be blown off course, and even if successfully fired it was a slow and cumbersome task to get the crew ashore. In 1920, for example, the *Maria Jose* went aground at Southerndown and Mr Cowie and Mr Deeble of Porthcawl had to go all round the coast in their horse and cart. They set up their equipment on the cliffs and at great risk to themselves carried out a successful rescue, although unfortunately the ship's cook became entangled in the ropes and had to be retrieved upside down. Although injured he was still alive when they got him ashore.

Rockets and Breeches Buoy were of no use when the *Samtampa* was driven aground at Sker in April 1947. Those alive today still remember that night with awe, for the storm was of an intensity rarely encountered even in the Bristol Channel. Rocket after rocket went adrift, although the ship seemed tantalisingly close to the shoreline. A Liberty ship, built in America by mass-production methods during the second World War, the huge freighter was being tossed about like a cork. The Mumbles lifeboat, *Edward Prince of Wales*, was quickly on the scene and onlookers watched anxiously as the small craft made repeated attempts to get near the stricken vessel. All to no avail, for the lifeboat capsized and all the crew of eight drowned. By the morning the *Samtampa* was already splitting into three sections, two of which were later lifted bodily on to the jagged rocks and all the crew of 39 perished as well. They were buried at the new Porthcawl cemetery. For many years after the tragedy the engine and boiler of the freighter could still be seen on the sands of Sker Beach, a long-lasting reminder of that dreadful night.

Fortunately no great loss of life has occurred in our area since that time. During the second World War an R.A.F. bomber-training station was built at Stormy Down, and throughout hostilities—and for some years afterwards— sea-rescue was undertaken by R.A.F. personnel and marine craft stationed in the old Jenning's building. Primarily to go to the aid of ditched airmen the Marine Section did great service rescuing anyone who was in difficulties on or near the Porthcawl coast, but when the station closed down the service craft were withdrawn. The Royal National Lifeboat Institution stepped in again and provided the resort with a new type of off-shore craft powered by outboard motors. The maroons are still heard frequently, especially in the summer months, and the response of the volunteer crews is still as immediate as it ever was; but now, fortunately, most of the incidents are concerned with bathers and small craft. Over-all guard of the coastline is still maintained by the crews of the Mumbles lifeboat, which has been carrying out this task ever since the *Speedwell* went out of service. And still the R.N.L.I. relies on the generosity of individual members of the community who delve deeply into their pockets regularly and unstintingly.

17.

Miscellaneous Information

A.   *The Brogden Family*

The Brogdens have been mentioned many times in the chapters dealing with the docks and the early town of Porthcawl but a short summary of that remarkable family is necessary to complete the picture. Like the majority of the entrepreneurs who developed the industries of South Wales in the nineteenth century the Brogdens were English, hailing originally from Lancashire. John Brogden, the head of the family firm, settled in Manchester in 1822 where his four children were born: John, Alexander, Henry and James. All the boys eventually became partners in the firm which was active in the building of railways and the mining of iron ore. Much of this ore was imported into South Wales to feed the furnaces then opening up and some of it came through the original small Porthcawl dock. It was this connection that first brought the Brogdens' attention to the area. In 1853 the firm purchased the Tondu Iron-works from Sir Robert Price and also the rights to mine coal and iron in the surrounding countryside. James Brogden, the junior partner, was put in charge of the undertaking and, because of his energy and enterprise, two blast furnaces, three rolling mills and many smaller furnaces came into successful production.

By 1860 the mining of coal was in full swing in the valleys to the north of Tondu, and it was not long before the Brogdens were sinking mines in the vicinity of Maesteg and Ogmore. In order to find an outlet for the coal the firm promoted the Ogmore Valley Railway Company, and it was this undertaking that brought the Brogden coal to Porthcawl. Soon it became necessary to enlarge the existing dock and once more James was put in charge. His work in this connection and his development of the new town has already been described, and so it only remains to record the subsequent vicissitudes of the family's fortunes.

John, the eldest son, died in his thirties in 1855 and so took little part in the South Wales undertakings; and when John Brogden senior died in 1869 Alexander assumed the position as head of the firm. He built Tondu House as the family residence (now a ruin) but for reasons best known to himself chose to reside in the vacant home of the co-respondent in his brother James' divorce case, then about to come to litigation. James, still living at Tondu House, greatly resented this, and the rift between the two brothers became so deep it affected the working of the firm. After completing the new dock at Porthcawl, but before he could get properly to grips with the building of the town, James was sent to New Zealand (1871) to build railways for the colonial government. He remained there for two years and during his absence Alexander consolidated his position as head of the firm, which then became known as the Llynvi, Tondu and Ogmore Coal and Iron Company, Ltd., with Henry as Managing Director. At that time the company possessed twelve collieries, nine blast furnaces and several forges and mills. The future of this formidable undertaking seemed assured. Unfortunately the Bessemer process and the importation of the superior Spanish ores was already making inroads into the company's profits, and in spite of all efforts to stave off disaster it failed. In 1878 a Receiver was called in. Further litigation over an Aberdare colliery finally put paid to matters and the Brogdens lost their industrial empire.

From then on the family's story is an unhappy one. Largely because of disputes over John Brogden senior's will, Alexander commenced an action against his two brothers and partners, Henry and James. It did not go to court but the subsequent bitterness brought about the dissolution of the partnership. Alexander left South Wales and James, having made a second and, as it turned out, a happy marriage to Mary Caroline Beete, niece of General Picton, settled in Sea Bank House with his new wife. Armed mainly with Mary's money the couple went on developing Porthcawl along the lines James had planned many years before, but the bad luck that had dogged the Brogden name struck again, this time finally. James and Mary Caroline lost all their money and had the ignominy of seeing their principal creation, the town of Porthcawl, taken over by other developers. James died in 1907, but not before being made fully aware of the esteem felt towards him, and his family, by the people of South Wales. At a meeting of the Ivorites Lodge, held at the Angel Inn, Aberkenfig, a song was sung to the tune of 'Merch Megan'. Its final verse reads as follows:

> May BROGDEN enjoy a long life of prosperity
>   In the hearts of the people and the favour of JOVE,
> Soon may he be married to an angel of goodness,
>   That will cheer him and help him in his labour of love;
> And may his descendants inherit his virtues—
>   His love of religion, his power of mind,
> His great liberality, integrity, and kindness,
>   His pleasure in lessening the ills of mankind.
> While the language of CYMRU be the language of Poets,
>   And bards to the virtuous sing their sweet lays,
> Our BROGDEN and all his magnanimous agents,
>   The country will ever resound with their praise.

21 James Brogden

B. *William Weston Young*

William Weston Young was another unlucky man. Like James Brogden he was kind, generous, affable, free from guile—and misfortune-prone. His impact on Newton-Nottage was not great like that of the industrialist but no history of the parish can be complete without reference to this remarkable person.

Although originally of Welsh stock Young was a Bristol man, born there in 1776 and brought up in the Quaker faith. His marriage to Elizabeth Davies, also a Quaker, was happy throughout its long existence. No one knows why, after many years of adventure, he chose to come to Wales in 1798 and lease a grist-mill at Aberdulais. There, with the bad luck that was to plague him for the rest of his life, a drought and bad harvests made him bankrupt by the age of 26. Having lost everything (including £1,000 borrowed from his wife) he became a 'draftsman' at the Cambrian Pottery in Swansea, earning £75 a year. There he put his artistic talents to work making engravings for a book and painting the famous Swansea pottery, but this was not enough to pay off his debts and so he turned to wreck-raising, an occupation that brought him to Newton-Nottage.

Previously wreck-raising and cargo-salvaging had been a hit or miss affair, but Young brought to the task an inventive mind and a capacity for detailed pre-planning. First he made a survey of the coast, calculating the number of wrecks that had occurred in the four great danger areas: the Black Rocks, the Tuskars, the Scarweather sand-shoal and Sker Point. The result appalled him, so he made a more detailed inventory of 39 ships wrecked off Newton between 1797 and 1818 and concentrated on those. He invented an ingenious grab to get at the cargoes and in the very first year he recovered copper from the *Anne and Teresa* which yielded a profit of £1,400. The winter weather brought a stop to this activity but Young, who could never remain still for long, except when sketching or painting, set up as a general merchant in Newton. This was no mere village shop but a fore-runner of today's super-store. Selling both wholesale and retail from a yard and a store-house the goods on sale were as diverse as Young's talents, including such things as oysters, cloth, rabbit skins, earthenware, ropes, spars and anchors. As a side-line he sold elm boards to make coffins, and for a while also resumed his first occupation of miller. Leasing the windmill on Newton Down, he ground the corn and sold it alongside all the other commodities. In the summer cargo-salvaging went on apace, work that made him realise to the full the dangerous life sailors led in the nineteenth century. This turned his thoughts to saving ships in distress, and so active did he become in this respect, and so eager to get to stricken vessels, he was accused of deliberate wrecking or at the very least furthering his career as a cargo raiser. Those who knew Young's generous nature refused to believe such accusations but some of the odium remained. The trouble with Young was that he could not spot a dishonest person when he saw one, and his trusting nature once more brought about a bankruptcy, causing him to seek and obtain the post of Official Surveyor of Roads in Glamorgan. Somehow he also found time to plan and create a marble tomb for Mansel Talbot in Margam Abbey, by which time everything he earned was going to the creditors.

His career then took another turn. Somehow obtaining more cash (usually from friends who liked him even if they doubted his business acumen) he became part owner of the Nantgarw pottery, where he helped produce the fine porcelain which are collectors' items today. This work took him away from Newton-Nottage for long periods but he did not lose contact with the parish for he set up a muffle-kiln at Newton where he fired some of the Nantgarw pottery. Unfortunately his partners absconded leaving him once more owing money all round, so he was forced to become a teacher of painting at Cowbridge Grammar School. That really ended his connection with our area and he went on to become successively (and sometimes simultaneously) an inventor of a chimney-furnace to destroy copper fumes (unsuccessful), an inventor of a silica brick for lining furnaces (so successful the bricks became known throughout the world although Young got no money out of his patent), the manager of a salt mine, the writer and engraver of a Guide to the Vale of Neath and a prolific artist, his work usually taking the form of pencil-sketches and water colours. His long-suffering but faithful wife died in 1842 and Young followed her five years later. Aged 71 he was impoverished to the end.

It is gratifying to record that this remarkable man was once a parishioner of Newton-Nottage.

C.   *The Rest Convalescent Home*

There are two popular misconceptions about the Convalescent Home at Rest Bay. One is that it was started by Florence Nightingale; the other is that its original purpose was to hospitalise Welsh miners. Both are false. The true account is as follows:

In 1849 the cholera epidemic was sweeping South Wales. In Maesteg Dr. James Lewis, F.R.C.S., L.R.C.P., who was the Medical Officer for both the Bridgend and Cowbridge Union and Messrs Brogdens' Mines and Colliery Company, was playing his part in the fight against the disease. When the worst of the epidemic had died down he became increasingly appalled by the poverty and illness largely caused by the aftermath of the scourge. The idea came to him to start a place where poor people could go for a week or so to recuperate, preferably away from the valleys which were then becoming increasingly industrialised. He decided on the new and growing town of Porthcawl which,

22   The Rest Convalescent Home in 1920

although it had a dock complex continuously hazy with coal dust, was still largely unspoiled. He obtained two cottages in New Road (then consisting of just a handful of houses) and knocked them together to form one building. Funded by money donated by benevolent land owners and industrialists whom Dr. Lewis, his wife and friends had approached, 73 patients came to stay for short periods and most of them benefited greatly from the pure sea air. The first Annual Report, published in 1863, showed how successful the scheme had been, and the residential home was given the name 'The Rest'. Later, when the large new building at Rest Bay was completed, the original place became known as 'The Old Rest' for it continued in being during and after the construction of the new home.

Within a few years it became obvious that the cottages in New Road were too small for the numbers wishing to recuperate there, so Dr. Lewis decided to create a much larger building, and the spot he chose was near a wide, sweeping bay with panoramic views all round and where the prevailing westerly wind was completely unpolluted. The actual site was generously given (freehold) by the Talbot family of Margam. Dr. James also wrote to Florence Nightingale seeking her advice as to the best type of building and having received it (her letter is still in The Rest archives) he obtained the services of the Diocesan architect, John Prichard. In 1874 the scheme was started using mountain limestone found on the site and a superior grade of the same stone obtained from a local quarry. By the 17th July 1878, The Rest was ready for its first invalid. Subsequently enlarged the fine Victorian building gave its name to the bay. Florence Nightingale continued to give her moral support but did not visit the site.

The new Rest Home continued along the lines of the old. Sick people or those recuperating from an illness who could not afford a holiday were invited to stay there. No distinction was made about their occupations but as the century progressed more and more miners succumbed to the deadly diseases of silicosis and emphysema and so many pit-men came to the home. This undoubtedly gave rise to the belief that The Rest was primarily a miners' hospital. Funding went on as before, for The Rest has never been affiliated to any organisation but is a charitable trust relying heavily on voluntary effort and contributions. The mining and other industries have always given their full support.

Today, thanks to Dr. James Lewis and people who still give generously, The Rest is as active as ever. It looks after the disabled, not only from Wales but from all over the United Kingdom. To meet changing needs the remaining large wards are being converted into double bedrooms. The long and constant battle to obtain funds goes on continuously.

D.   Inns and Public Houses

Mention has already been made of Porthcawl's early hostelries but as there were at least 31 in the parish in 1866 it would be of interest to many to reiterate their names and positions.

Newton has the distinction of possessing the first licensed premises in the parish. This was the Jolly Sailor which came into being when Newton was a port. At first it was a brew-house, certainly in being by 1818, owned by a David Jones who was a carpenter in the village. Even by then it had developed a reputation as being something of a smugglers' headquarters—no doubt true in view of the fact that the lords of the manor exacted dues on every cargo being landed at Newton Weir. Later it was joined by the Crown Inn (now Crown House) also situated on the perimeter of the village green and a few years later by the Ancient Briton. The name of the latter inn was changed to the Newton Hotel before reverting to its old title. On the other side of the village the Globe Inn was built near a large pool, an overflow from the Newton Waun. Another inn, the Welcome to Town, was just a small cottage adjoining Hope Chapel on the Newton-Nottage Road. Even after it had closed down its sign could be seen from the road for many years afterwards. Finally there was a beer house called the Harriet (named after one of the daughters of the Knight family) at the foot of Clevis Hill, but it was burned down and replaced by the first Newton National School.

Not to be out-done Nottage, in spite of being a bastion of nonconformity, could boast of five public houses. One of the earliest was the New Moon, situated on the square in the middle of the village. Although no longer in existence it was soon joined by the Farmers' Arms—aptly named in view of the fact that for centuries Nottage has been the centre of a farming community—and the Swan Inn. The writer has never been able to ascertain whether the latter place was named after the bird or the Swan family who owned much land in and around the village in the nineteenth century. No doubt exists about the Rose and Crown Inn, which was created out of two old cottages, Rose Cottage and Crown Cottage, the latter being the original ale house. Before becoming the superior establishment it is today the Rose and Crown was run by Mrs Mabel Roberts whose boast was that she served the best pint in the area and that she had never left Nottage. Another beer house which has disappeared was the Lamb Inn, situated on the hill leading to the main Cornelly road. It was converted into No. 1 and No. 2 Lamb Cottages, also subsequently demolished, their place being taken by The Garden Cottage.

The first public house in Porthcawl did not appear until the first dock was started in 1828, and then several sprang up in the vicinity of the dockside to cater for the thirst of men working in the coal-dust laden atmosphere. Mostly they were converted private houses—converted at an indecent speed according to the chapel-goers of the time. One of the first was the Knight's Arms, open to customers in 1830, and still on its original site. It was closely followed by the Harbour Inn, now Ye Pirates' Club, the Ship and Castle, the Ship Aground (on the site of the present Pier Hotel), the Anchor Inn (later a cafe but subsequently demolished to make way for the present Glamorgan Holiday Home) and the General Picton. The latter place had originally been Eastner Cottage, situated

23   The Harbour Inn, now Ye Pirates' Club

within the early dock complex, but later the tavern moved to its present position in New Road and the cottage was demolished.

As Porthcawl grew in size and the second dock came into operation many other licensed premises appeared. One was the Victoria Inn, built at the junction of Victoria Avenue and John Street. Later it moved to a site at the top of Station Hill and, to avoid confusion among imbibers, the original building was re-named the Rock Hotel. The second Victoria Inn, or rather Victoria Hotel as it came to be known, was demolished when plans for the Portway and the shopping precinct were finalised. Further along Old Station Lane was the Three Horse Shoes, but that, too, was demolished, its place being taken by cottages. Two other taverns in close proximity were the Royal Oak (originally a beer-house) and the New Inn, later renamed the Sea Horse. Also on South Road were the Railway Inn and the Star Inn, two establishments which eventually reverted to their original roles as residential cottages.

Along New Road there were no less than eleven public houses towards the end of the nineteenth century. In addition to the Victoria Hotel and the General Picton there were (and still are) the Prince of Wales, the Queen's Hotel (once also the changing place for the Porthcawl Rugby Club whose pitch was nearby), the Mackworth Arms (named after the famous copper magnate) and the Brogden Hotel. Other hostelries which went out of existence at various times were the Albion Inn (which became the Osborne Cafe and eventually a shop), the Masons' Arms (now the New Road Sub-post Office), the White

Lion (at 117 New Road), the Greyhound (opposite the old pumping station in Mackworth Road) and, according to the older inhabitants of the parish, the Carpenters' Arms which once occupied the site of The Vineries. As though all these establishments were not enough there was also a number of beer-houses such as the Golden Key, a few of them brewing their own beer, but as the existence of many was fleeting they have not been included in this brief account.

In addition there were four early hotels licensed to sell intoxicating liquor. One of the first was the Porthcawl Hotel, premises built during the early stages of the construction of John Street in the eighteen-eighties and subsequently enlarged. James Brogden also built the Esplanade Hotel, constructed in a manner which made conversion into private houses possible should the venture fail. It did not fail and when R. E. Jones undertook the development of part of the town after Brogden's bankruptcy he turned it into one of the resort's premier hotels. Sea Bank House, where James Brogden and his family resided, became a school when the financial crash came. Known as Porthcawl College it was later bought by John Elias who turned it into a private unlicensed hotel before re-selling it to a company which made it into a much bigger place. It did not have a licence until the inter-war years and then only after an appeal by the manager for the support of the Royal Porthcawl Golf Club because so many golfers were staying at the hotel. The appeal was successful and the Seabank went on to become the biggest and most important of Porthcawl's hotels. Finally there was the Marine Hotel, also built by James Brogden when the Promenade was being constructed. It went through many vicissitudes before part of the building once more became a licensed premises, happily reviving an old parish hostelry name—the Anchor.

E. *The Paddle Steamers*

Between the two World Wars many paddle steamers graced the Bristol Channel much to the delight of Porthcawlians and the many holiday makers who came to the resort. Sailing regularly from the breakwater day-trips could be made to such places as Ilfracombe, Minehead, Lundy, etc. Sunday was the most popular day for outings, for the Sunday Closing Act of the time forbade the sale of intoxicating liquor in the town's many hostelries, and the ships' bars were open as soon as the vessels were under way. Few people know, however, that the first paddle steamers arrived in the Bristol Channel as early as 1887.

The home of this particular type of vessel was the Clyde, the original *Waverley* entering service with P. and A. Campbell in 1884. The managing director of the firm, the late Sir Alec Campbell, decided to try her out in the Bristol Channel and so successful was the venture that the White Funnel Fleet was formed with several additional steamers. Their names became familiar at ports and resorts on both sides of the Channel. They were the *Ravenswood* (commissioned 1891), the *Westward Ho* (1894), and the *Cambria* (1895). In the next fifteen years other vessels joined the fleet: *Britannia, Lady Ismay, Glen Avon,*

24 P. and A. Campbell paddle steamer at the Breakwater

Glen Usk, Brighton Queen, Albion and *Glen Rosa*. Later (1911) three more were
purchased: the *Devonia, Barry* and *Westonia*. This brought the total number of
vessels to fourteen by the outbreak of the first World War.

As soon as war was declared all the steamers were commandeered by the
navy and served throughout hostilities under the White Ensign, mostly as
mine-sweepers. Two were lost in action (*Lady Ismay* and *Brighton Queen*) and
the ravages of war-service made three (including the *Waverley*) unusable for
channel service which was resumed in 1919. The firm went on sailing with the
remaining craft, changed the name of the *Barry* to *Waverley* (an unlucky omen
the sailors said), ordered a new steamer, the *Glen Gower*, and purchased two
much older vessels, the *Lady Moyra* and *Lady Evelyn*. The last two were
renamed *Brighton Queen* and *Brighton Belle*—unlucky again as it turned out.
With this revitalised fleet came the hey-day of the paddle steamer in the Bristol
Channel.

War came again in 1939 and once more the vessels were commandeered by
the navy. All three renamed steamers were lost in action as were the *Devonia*
and *Glen Gower*. In addition the *Westward Ho* and the *Cambria* were in such a
poor condition they had to be scrapped. This reduced the fleet to five so two
more ships were ordered, the *Cardiff Queen* (1946) and the *Bristol Queen* (1947).
These were the last of the paddle steamers, for diesel power was ousting steam
and the next three ships commissioned were also diesel: the *St Trillo*, the
Westward Ho and the *Balmoral*. Nevertheless the fastest ship in the fleet was still a

paddle steamer, the *Britannia*, which could do 21 knots and once made the crossing from Penarth to Weston in 29 minutes.

By now, however, the Severn Bridge had been built and holiday habits were changing. This was the age of the motor car and foreign holidays and so the demand for day-trips in the channel grew less. The last of the paddle steamers, the *Queens*, ceased to operate and by 1981 only the *Balmoral* was being used. The Campbell steamers had been in existence for 94 years. Now the only link with the past is provided by the Paddle Steamer Preservation Society which, after the loss of the *Ivanhoe* off the Gower coast, continues to sail its own *Waverley* (now the last paddle steamer in the world) and the motor ship *Balmoral*. Regretfully excursions from the Porthcawl breakwater are now fewer in number, but the two vessels continue to provide a nostalgic link with what once has been.

F.   *The Porthcawl Aerodrome*

To say that Porthcawl once had an aerodrome during the inter-war years would be an exaggeration, for the landing area consisted of only a field, the odd tent and caravan, and at night the aircraft were tied down with ropes in case a gust of wind blew them over. This did not discourage the *Daily Herald* from proclaiming in 1936 that 'a new airport for Porthcawl would serve the purpose of air travel to London and the Midlands' and that 'the resort was now on the airways map'. Thus from the earliest days the field abutting Locks Lane (still there and now growing a variety of crops) was referred to by Porthcawlians as 'The Aerodrome', and the person responsible for starting this enterprise was the late Mr George Pine, M.B.E.

To obtain his first aeroplane Mr Pine, a local garage owner and caravan salesman, saved up for 26 years, and the machine he ultimately purchased was a 130 hp. de Haviland Fox Moth with a Gipsy Major engine capable of carrying four passengers as well as the pilot (who sat in an open cockpit). Although he had already served in the R.F.C. and A.C.C., Mr Pine had to obtain a commercial flying licence and, armed with this, he began operating a taxi service to Swansea and Cardiff. In between flights there were trips around the bay for 5s (25p) with a straight 'up and down' for 2s 6d (12½p). So successful was the venture that a second aircraft was soon obtained, and even in the days of the Great Depression there were enough passengers to keep the business viable. Both aeroplanes had a number of hair-raising adventures ranging from such things as 'prangs' with the field's surrounding walls, leading an R.A.F. bomber lost in a fog to a safe rendezvous at Porthcawl's flying field, and a forced landing near Margam. Mr Pine was also employed by the War Office to 'bomb' army convoys during exercises to ascertain the effect of aircraft on troop move-ments—a forerunner of events in the forthcoming war. Occasionally 'the aerodrome' was used by travelling flying circuses which put on aerobatic displays much to the enjoyment of townspeople and holiday makers, and there

25 Mr George Pine's Fox Moth and bathing beauties.
A promotion photograph

were also exhibitions of exotica such as cars which had broken the world land-speed record, namely Sir Henry Seagrave's Golden Arrow and Kaye Don's Silver Bullet. No doubt because of all this successful activity flying operations in the town would have gone on expanding, but in 1939 came the outbreak of war. Mr Pine enlisted as a pilot with an Air Transport Auxiliary Squadron, ferrying aircraft from America and between aerodromes in Britain. Sadly, after the war the business was not resumed and the flying field reverted to agricultural use.

G. *Nottage Tunnel and the Porthcawl Breakwater*

When the original tramroad to the Porthcawl dock was constructed its route ran just to the east of Nottage (a newer section in the stonework of the wall of Nottage Court indicates the direction it went) and as long as the trams were horse-drawn no objection was raised. But when the line was converted to use by steam locomotives in the eighteen-sixties farmers and land-owners were afraid that the noise of these new-fangled monsters would frighten cattle and that ash from their boilers might set crops alight. There was nothing unusual in this, for it happened throughout Britain. A new route to the west would have been difficult to construct because of the terrain, and in any case would have run across agricultural land, so there was only one way to go—through or under Nottage. The first course being deemed impracticable it was decided to make a short tunnel extending from the northern perimeter of the village to just beyond the outlying barns and buildings in the south. Along this single line of track went the freight trains carrying coal and iron to the now busy dock complex and when the dock was finally closed the line became Porthcawl's only railway connection with the hinterland. It was quite a busy line taking early morning businessmen's trains direct to Cardiff, and a special little station—Nottage Halt—was built for the convenience of golfers going to play at the Royal Porthcawl Golf Club. For most passengers, however, there was the inevitable change at Pyle Junction to catch the main line trains. The tunnel itself became a great joy to children on the many excursion trains that came to Porthcawl in the inter-war years, for they knew that once through its smoky confines they would be within sight and sound of the sea. The tunnel also caused consternation to motorists when they found themselves engulfed in clouds of smoke and steam on entering the village. Most Porthcawlians thought it a sad day when the Beeching 'axe' did away with this branch line, for the resort became dependent on road transport which could be badly affected in snowy conditions. The tunnel was blocked up at both ends and Porthcawl lost a memorable, if somewhat bizarre, attraction.

At the terminus of the early railway was the Porthcawl Dock which was able to operate only because of the shelter afforded by the breakwater. When the original small dock was constructed in the lee of Porth Cawl Point a short defensive wall was built to protect the entrance to the harbour, but when the second, much larger, dock came into operation this defence line proved inadequate, so James Brogden extended the structure one hundred yards out to sea. To look at the massive stonework today it is difficult to believe that it is hollow along part of its length. This is because a skeleton of massive oak beams and cross-struts was first erected, the men employed on this task coming mainly from the Forest of Dean. This had the dual purpose of acting as a support for the subsequent installation of the huge stone blocks and also to give the entire structure a degree of elasticity against the ferocious strength of wind and waves. Close inspection of these blocks, hewn at local quarries, will reveal the skill with which the masons put them together. It is also remarkable that all this work was done using nothing more powerful than hand-winches and block-and-tackle. To protect the wall facing the prevailing south-west wind an escarpment of equally large stone blocks was laid, and this has undoubtedly been the main reason for the longevity of the entire structure. Although the breakwater has to be periodically repaired and refaced it has stood the test of time for over a century, a remarkable testimony to the men who built it.

When the breakwater was completed it became necessary to construct a beacon at its extremity. Tenders were put out and the successful firm was Messrs. Stephen of Bristol. The first lantern, which was oil-fired, went up in

26   Porthcawl's first lighthouse completed in 1865

1865 and from the beginning it showed a continuous light. Unfortunately the top was washed off the twenty foot high structure in 1911, and when a new top was added (the one that is still there today) advantage was taken of the opportunity to install gas lighting, and this is the method of illumination still in use today. The little lighthouse now guides only small craft into the harbour but it has become a much-loved emblem of the resort.

H.   *Royal Porthcawl Golf Club and Nottage Halt*

In 1891 a group of Cardiff professional and business men decided to form a golf club, and the name they selected was St David. Then came the opportunity of leasing Porthcawl's Locks Common, which would form the basis of a good links course, so 'Porthcawl Golf Club' was settled on instead, the first President being Sir Morgan Morgan. A nine-hole course was laid out (older members maintain they can still see where the greens and fairways were) and a club house erected on a grassy sward near the present 'Ocean View'. Unfortunately the common was also used in the summer months by the forerunner of today's Territorial Army, known as The Volunteers, and so during part of July and August the golfers had to stop playing and allow the soldiers to take over. Hundreds of tents were erected and holes dug for latrines and field kitchens—something which must have caused premature ageing among early committee members. Dressed in red tunics and spiked helmets the soldiers were also continually drilling and marching but, surprisingly, they and the golfers got on well together, so much so that in 1895 the officers of the Severn Volunteer Brigade presented the club with a trophy in recognition of the inconvenience caused to members. Known as the Severn Brigade Shield this handsome trophy is still competed for today. Another trophy presented in 1895 was the Brogden Bowl, given by James Brogden, one of the founder members who had also done so much for Porthcawl.

In spite of the good relations that existed between the club and the military it became imperative to find a new site, and the opportunity came when land for the present eighteen-hole links course was offered on lease. The club house was dismantled and taken to its present position, and members settled down to enjoy their new amenities. In 1909 the club was honoured by having the title 'Royal' conferred on it by Edward VII.

The entrance to the new course was then via a metalled track leading from South Road, and as many members lived in Cardiff and other parts of the county the G.W.R. was approached with a view to building a small railway station on the branch line at Nottage. This was done and Nottage Halt came into being primarily for golfers, although later it was also much used by commuters going to Cardiff on the special businessmen's trains. One of the top G.W.R. officials (a keen golfer himself) gave strict instructions that a train must halt there even if there was only one member of the club aboard. This being the era before motor cars there was always a horse and trap waiting at the halt to take players to the course. Over the years the greens and fairways were steadily improved until 'The Royal' became one of the foremost links courses in Britain, attracting not only individual golfers but many national and international events of world-wide prestige. In 1960 the club was able to purchase the freehold of the course and the boring of an artesian well near the tenth tee ensured a constant supply of water even in times of severe drought.

I. *The Police*

The Glamorgan Constabulary was established in 1839 and expanded a year later to cover the entire county. Porthcawl fell into the Bridgend District which in its early days was policed by a Superintendent and three constables. As the town of Porthcawl grew in size around the dock complex it was deemed necessary that the parish should have its own police station, and a site for its construction was reserved in a central position in John Street. When the western side of the street was built up in the eighteen eighties the first police station therefore had a prime position, becoming a substantial Victorian structure complete with blue lamp, lock-up cubicles and a 'prisoners' yard'. The first constables were Thomas Protheroe (1880), William Williams (1891) and Thomas Hywel Jenkins (1920). Their task must have been difficult for the dockers and sailors of those days were not always amenable to discipline, especially after they had been imbibing in one of the town's many taverns. Between the wars the force was led by a sergeant but after the amalgamation in 1969, when the Glamorgan constabulary became the South Wales Constabulary, it was obvious that the original station was both unsuitable and too small to cater for a continuously expanding population, augmented in the summer months by many thousands of holiday-makers and day-trippers. A decision was made in 1973 to sell the building to Ogwr Borough Council and a new police station was erected opposite Trinity Church. Today Porthcawl is a Sub-Divisional Headquarters station for 'F' or Brigend Division, and is under the control of a Chief Inspector.

The old building was renovated by Ogwr Borough Council and put to good use, becoming a Town Information Centre, a display area for paintings and drawings by members of the Porthcawl Arts Society and the headquarters of Porthcawl Museum and Historical Society. Evidence still remains of the lock-up cubicles, although the special top-secret locks were removed by order of the Home Office. The prisoners' exercise yard is still open to the skies but plans are afoot to roof the area so that the Museum will have additional space to display its exhibits.

J. Picture Gallery

27 New House. Later it became Porthcawl College and then
the Seabank Hotel

28 James Brogden's original sea wall in 1886. Seabank House left, centre, Lias Cottages in the distant fields

29 The Promenade and the Esplanade Hotel, completed 1887

30 The Sea-front and the Pier Hotel. Jutting out, centre, is
the lifeboat station

31   Pre-World War I fashions

32   A leisurely chat in the middle of the promenade, about 1912.
Centre, the Victorian shelter

33 The promenade looking eastward, circa 1914

34 The watch house and look-out tower. The gun was a trophy captured
from the Germans in the 1914-18 War

Old Watch House
Round Tower
and Lighthouse

35 The inner dock gates, completed in 1867

36   The inner dock in 1890. Within a few years the undertaking had failed

37 The first Victoria Avenue, completed by 1914. The Victoria Inn was situated at its junction with John Street

38 John Street looking north. The Porthcawl Hotel is on the right, the Post Office on the left

39 John Street before the motor-car era

40 Territorial Army soldiers marching down an uncompleted John Street in 1907. The bay-fronted house is in Lias Road

41 Porthcawl's first railway station in South Road. Later it was demolished and a new station built at the end of the present Portway

42 The second railway station. It ceased to function when the Beeching 'axe' did away with many branch lines in the nineteen-sixties

43 The level-crossing gates. The Victoria Hotel is on the left

44 Children's paddling pool in the nineteen-thirties. By then the Seabank Hotel had been greatly enlarged

45 The Salt Lake. Between the wars it was a popular attraction
for swimmers and boaters

46 The Slip. The bridge and wooden jetty were still standing when this
picture was taken in 1930

47 Coney Beach about 1925. The 'Shelter' was a converted World War I aeroplane hangar

48 Rest Bay with bathing huts. In the nineteen-twenties it was considered immodest to undress in public

88470 *Porthcawl, Nottage Well, 1938*

49 Nottage Avenue and Ffynnon Fawr

50 Stoneleigh College. The iron fountain in the wall now graces the shelter near the Seabank Hotel

STONELEIGH COLLEGE

51 Skating Carnival, 1933. At one time there were no less than three roller skating rinks at Cosy Corner

52 The Cosy Corner Cinema, 1935

53   The Lower Promenade under construction, 1934

54   St David's Day at the National School. Author is left, back row,
Mr Phillip Aspinal sitting, left

K. *Porthcawl clubs and Societies*

R.N.L.I.
Disabled Group
Olde Tyme Dancing
1st Porthcawl Boys' Brigade
1st Porthcawl Girls' Brigade
2nd Porthcawl Girls' Brigade
Harbour Boating Club
Sea Cadets
Townswomen's Guild
Power and Ski Club
Awel y Mor Old Tyme Dancing
1st Nottage Scout Group
Awel y Mor Bridge Club
Awel y Mor O.A.P. Association
Nottage Keep Fit Club
Porthcawl Scout Group
Girl Guides
Porthcawl School of Judo
Porthcawl School of Yoga
St John Ambulance
A.T.C.
Cricket Club
Hockey Club
Floral Arrangement Society
Horticultural Society
Junior and Senior Youth Clubs
Porthcawl A.F.C. (Juniors)
Porthcawl A.F.C. (Seniors)
Porthcawl Fencing Club
Porthcawl Rugby Club
Cancer Research Society
Red Cross
Blood Donor Group
Porthcawl Oxfam Group
Spastics Aid Society
Mentally Handicapped Society
Kidney Research
Inner Wheel
R.N.L.I. Ladies' Section
W.R.V.S.
N.S.P.C.C.
Archery Group
Porthcawl Choral Society
Wesley Youth Club
All Saints' Singers

Porthcawl & Pyle Amateur
    Athletic Society
All Saints' Youth Group
Save the Children Fund
Lions Club of Porthcawl
British Legion
Porthcawl Arts Society
Museum and Historical Society
Porthcawl Little Theatre
Women's Advisory Council
Cymdeithas Cymraeg
Merched y Wawr
Citizens' Advice Bureau
Chamber of Trade
41 Club
Porthcawl Lifeguard Club
Ladies' Section Rugby Club
Round Table
Round Table Ladies' Section
Rotary Club
R.A.F.A.
Loyal Order of the Moose
Y.M.C.A.
Porthcawl Operatic Society
Porthcawl & District Tourist
    Association
Porthcawl Civic Trust Society
Newton Institute
Horse Show Society
Porthcawl Male Choir
Nutters Charity Group
People and Piano
Porthcawl Music Club
Ladies' Catholic League
Sea Angling Society
L.A.T.C.H.
P.R.O.B.U.S.
The League of Friends
Nottage W.I.
Newton W.I.
Sker W.I.
Royal Porthcawl Golf Club
Porthcawl Wednesday Club
Newtonian Bowling Club
Griffin Park Bowling Club

Index